UNDERSTANDING THE FREE-WILL CONTROVERSY

CASCADE COMPANIONS

The Christian theological tradition provides an embarrassment of riches: from Scripture to modern scholarship, we are blessed with a vast and complex theological inheritance. And yet this feast of traditional riches is too frequently inaccessible to the general reader.

The Cascade Companions series addresses the challenge by publishing books that combine academic rigor with broad appeal and readability. They aim to introduce nonspecialist readers to that vital storehouse of authors, documents, themes, histories, arguments, and movements that comprise this heritage with brief yet compelling volumes.

SOME OTHER TITLES IN THIS SERIES:

Cascade Companion to Evil by Charles Taliaferro
Metaphysics by Donald Wallenfang
Phenomenology by Donald Wallenfang
Virtue by Olli-Pekka Vainio
Reading Paul by Michael Gorman
The Rule of Faith by Everett Ferguson
The Second-Century Apologists by Alvyn Pettersen
Origen by Ronald E. Heine
Athanasius of Alexandria by Lois Farag
Practicing Lament by Rebekah Eklund
Forgiveness: A Theology by Anthony Bash
Called to Attraction: The Theology of Beauty by Brendan T. Sammon
A Primer in Ecotheology by Celia Deane-Drummond
Postmodern Theology by Carl Raschke
Jacques Ellul by Jacob E. Van Vleet and Jacob M. Rollinson
Understanding Pannenberg by Anthony C. Thiselton
The Becoming of God: Process Theology by Ronald Faber
Theology and Science Fiction by James F. McGrath
The U.S. Immigration Crisis by Miguel de la Torre
Feminism and Christianity by Caryn Riswold
Theological Theodicy by Daniel Castelo
Creationism and the Conflict over Evolution by Tatha Wiley
Queer Theology by Linn Marie Tonstad

UNDERSTANDING THE FREE-WILL CONTROVERSY

Thinking through a Philosophical Quagmire

THOMAS TALBOTT

 CASCADE *Books* · Eugene, Oregon

UNDERSTANDING THE FREE-WILL CONTROVERSY
Thinking through a Philosophical Quagmire

Cascade Companions

Cascade Books
An Imprint of Wipf and Stock Publishers
199 W. 8th Ave., Suite 3
Eugene, OR 97401

www.wipfandstock.com

PAPERBACK ISBN: 978-1-7252-6836-4
HARDCOVER ISBN: 978-1-7252-6837-1
EBOOK ISBN: 978-1-7252-6838-8

Cataloguing-in-Publication data:

Names: Talbott, Thomas [author]

Title: Understanding the free-will controversy : thinking through a
philosophical quagmire / Thomas Talbott.

Description: Eugene, OR: Cascade Books, 2022 | Series: Cascade Com-
panions | Includes bibliographical references and index.

Identifiers: ISBN 978-1-7252-6836-4 (paperback) | ISBN 978-1-7252-
6837-1 (hardcover) | ISBN 978-1-7252-6838-8 (ebook)

Subjects: LCSH: Free will and determinism | Free will and determin-
ism—Religious aspects—Christianity | Philosophy | Philosophy and
religion

Classification: BJ1461 T35 2022 (paperback) | BJ1461 (ebook)

VERSION NUMBER 08/15/22

I dedicate this book to all of my former students at Willamette University, who not only put up with me, but were in fact the joy of my life during my thirty-four years of teaching there.

CONTENTS

INTRODUCTION

PEOPLE USE THE TERM "free will" in a variety of different contexts, some very practical and others highly theoretical. As an illustration of the former kind of context, suppose that a man who commits a serious crime is caught by the police and then signs a letter of confession; suppose further that a lawyer or a judge should subsequently ask, "Did you sign this confession of your own free will?" The practical question being asked here would probably be something like, "Were you *coerced* into signing this confession?"—or, "Was this something you really wanted to do?" But these latter questions can easily lead to questions of a more theoretical nature. For suppose that, had this man not been caught with overwhelming evidence against him and had he not been facing serious prison time, he would never have confessed to his crime in the first place. Could we not then say that the total situation, including his strong desire for a reduced sentence, did indeed coerce his confession? Would this be any less coercive than someone placing a gun to my head and thereby shaping my willingness to do something that I would not otherwise have been willing to do?

We thus approach the *philosophical* problem of free will, free choice, and free action, which includes a vast array of complicated and vigorously disputed issues. But just what is the relevant freedom we are talking about here? It is generally thought to be the kind of freedom that moral responsibility requires, and one way to begin clarifying this freedom would be to identify conditions sometimes thought to be incompatible with it. Not everyone, of course, agrees that we humans are morally responsible for our actions. But even those philosophers who reject the idea of moral responsibility altogether typically hold that the requisite freedom either does not or cannot obtain. In any case, most people would agree, I presume, that the relevant freedom is incompatible with certain kinds of brain damage, serious mental illness, lack of normal mental development, or some level of coercion. Beyond that, however, a host of disagreements appear to be more intractable: for example, disagreements over various claims that the relevant freedom is incompatible with determinism, or incompatible with indeterminism, or incompatible with divine foreknowledge, or even incompatible with the assumption that certain propositions about the future have a definite truth value.

Although many of these disagreements may *appear* to be intractable, some of them, as we shall see, turn out to be mere *verbal disputes* rather than *real disputes* over some matter of substance. A verbal dispute, as some philosophers would call it, arises when two conditions obtain: (i) the disputing parties use a crucial term, such as "free will," in very different (or even slightly different) senses, and (ii) clarifying these different senses will reveal no real disagreement over some genuine matter of substance. Because such verbal disputes often arise within the context of a larger difference in overall perspective or even worldview, I do not mean to trivialize them altogether. But so long as one continues treating a verbal dispute about free will as if it were a real dispute, it becomes much harder to clarify the deeper differences in overall perspective that sometimes underlie such a dispute. Accordingly, I shall periodically expand upon these points in this volume

Beyond that, my main purpose in the chapters that follow is twofold: first, to clarify for an audience of educated non-specialists some of the issues that often arise in philosophical disputes over the existence and the nature of human free will, and second, to articulate what seems to me the most plausible perspective to adopt on these issues. In the first chapter, which is entitled "A Philosophical Quagmire," we'll identify what some of these specific issues are, the most basic (and well known) of which is the issue of whether free will is, or is not, compatible with determinism. Then, in the following two chapters, we'll examine, respectively, an influential argument that free will is incompatible with determinism and an equally influential argument that free will is incompatible with indeterminism. That should at least raise the question of whether the concept of free will is simply incoherent, a question that we shall address directly in chapter 4, which will also set forth what seems to me the most plausible way to understand the concept of free will. And finally, with a specific conception of freedom in hand, we can then consider two slightly more technical issues: whether the relevant freedom is incompatible with the assumption that all genuine propositions about the future have a truth value (chapter 5), and whether it is incompatible with divine foreknowledge (chapter 6). Although I know of no good reason to accept either of these incompatibilities, the conception of freedom set forth in chapter 4 should help to explain why an omnipotent and perfectly loving Creator of the universe, if one should exist, would have no need to rely upon either foreknowledge or what many now call middle knowledge (see chapter 6) in order to control our lives providentially and to guarantee a glorious end for his creation.

One final point. It is no more my intention in this short book to reference every philosopher who has made an important contribution to the issues discussed here than this would be my intention in an undergraduate philosophy course on free will. But even though it is not my intention here to advance cutting-edge scholarship on this topic, it is my intention, as I have said, to set forth a perspective that will inevitably reflect some of my own conclusions about the nature and the existence of human freedom. The reflections contained herein will also include some ideas and even some language in a few cases from the following previously published material:

"Heaven and Hell in Christian Thought." In *The Stanford Encyclopedia of Philosophy* (Summer 2021 ed.), edited by Edward N. Zalta. https://plato.stanford.edu/archives/sum2021/entries/heaven-hell/.

"Grace, Character Formation, and Predestination unto Glory." In *The Problem of Hell: A Philosophical Anthology*, edited by Joel Buenting, 7–27. Burlington, VT: Ashgate, 2010.

"God, Freedom, and Human Agency." *Faith and Philosophy* 26 (2009) 378–97.

"Why Christians Should *Not* Be Determinists: Reflections on the Origin of Human Sin." *Faith and Philosophy* 25 (2008) 300–316.

"Indeterminism and Chance Occurrences." *The Personalist* 60 (1975) 253–61.

The book also includes one paragraph, slightly altered, from *The Inescapable Love of God*.

1

A PHILOSOPHICAL QUAGMIRE

ONE OF THE MOST persistent controversies with respect to free will concerns its compatibility, or incompatibility, with causal determinism. Not surprisingly, those who believe that free will and determinism are compatible typically call themselves *compatibilists* and those who disagree with this typically call themselves *incompatibilists*. But just how should we understand the idea of *causal determinism* in the context of this controversy?

THE THESIS OF DETERMINISM

A specific event is causally determined when it is the product of sufficient causes that render its nonoccurrence causally impossible. More generally, the thesis of determinism is the thesis that every event that occurs in time is the product of such sufficient causes; so if this thesis should be true, then all of our choices would be traceable to sufficient causes that lie either in the distant past before we were born or in eternity itself. There is, of course, more than one way in which this thesis might be true. An atheist who believes in determinism might hold that the Big Bang (setting aside any question concerning its own explanation) "quickly" resulted in a set of conditions and laws of nature such that from a complete description of both these early conditions and the laws of nature governing them the entire future course of the universe, including every human action, was in principle deducible. A *theological* determinist, by way of contrast, might hold that many events—specific miracles, for example, and related instances of divine interference in the created order—cannot be explained by an appeal to the laws of nature alone. Still, such divine interferences in the created order, or miraculous occurrences if you prefer, would hardly qualify as uncaused occurrences.

Now the Calvinist philosopher, Jonathan Edwards, seems clearly to have accepted this thesis of determinism, arguing that "nothing can ever happen without a [sufficient] cause or a reason why it occurs thus rather than so," and he then went on to remark, "I have especially produced evidence for this in connection with acts of the will."[1] But even if it should turn out that not *every* event is causally determined, the question of the ultimate springs of human action would yet remain. A determinist with respect to human behavior, for example, might nonetheless accept indeterminism on the quantum level, or even accept the idea that a dog's leaping this way rather than that while romping in the yard is not precisely determined. For the crucial issue in the present context concerns *human* behavior: how we should assess those cases where someone's action is the product of sufficient causes that lie outside this person's ultimate control. Accordingly, the thesis of determinism is

1. Edwards, *Freedom of the Will*, Part 2, Sec. 8.

a convenient way of assuming, for the sake of a given argument, that all of our actions are indeed the product of such sufficient causes.

COMPATIBILISM VERSUS INCOMPATIBILISM

Although compatibilists hold that free will and determinism are quite compatible, as the name itself implies, no compatibilist would claim that *every* causally determined action, no matter what its cause (or causes) may be, will qualify as an instance of someone acting freely. So the trick, according to compatibilists, is to distinguish between those causally determined actions that do and those that do not qualify as free actions. Virtually all compatibilists would thus insist that acting freely requires a freedom from compulsion and obsession (of a psychiatric kind), constraint of some specifiable kinds, and the *experience* of being coerced against one's own will. Where these (and perhaps some additional) conditions are met, one then acts freely in a given situation whenever one does what one most wants to do in that situation. In any such a case as this, a person retains the power, many of the early compatibilists in particular would insist, to act otherwise in the following *conditional sense*: if this person had not wanted to do this particular thing in this particular situation, then he or she would not have done it. Whenever one's own desires, motives, or intentions control one's own actions, after all, a radically different set of desires, motives, or intentions might clearly have resulted in a different action.

Lest there be any confusion in the matter, I should perhaps also point out that a compatibilist need not treat this conditional analysis as if it were, all by itself, a *sufficient condition* of someone's having the power to act otherwise in the compatibilist sense; much less would it qualify as a sufficient condition of someone's acting freely. For a genuine sufficient condition would also require that some additional conditions be met, such as an absence of irrational compulsion or obsession of a psychiatric kind. As the twentieth-century compatibilist P. H. Nowell-Smith once commented, "It is not an accident that we use 'compulsion' in a psychological way to exonerate compulsives"—particularly when their compulsions are not responsive to rational considerations.[2] Or, to borrow an example from Timothy O'Connor and Christopher Franklin,[3] if someone suffers from agoraphobia—an irrational fear of open spaces—and what one most wants to do in a given situation is to avoid these open spaces, then this person may not be free to do otherwise in the compatibilist sense even when the conditional analysis, taken by itself, might seem to suggest such freedom. Of course, trying to assess what an agoraphobic most wants to do can itself be rather tricky; some may desperately wish that they could go outside, only to discover that they cannot do so. But we can let that pass. For the point is that one should always think of the compatibilist's conditional analysis as presupposing a context in which certain kinds of irrationality, compulsion, and obsession have already been excluded.

According to incompatibilists, by way of contrast, free will could never exist in a fully deterministic universe because performing an action freely requires, at the very least, that the one who performs it must be its ultimate source in the sense that nothing external to this agent, such as a set of conditions that existed long before the agent was even born, was causally sufficient for it. Free will also requires, therefore, a universe in which alterative actions and different courses of events are both *causally* possible. But even

2. Nowell-Smith, *Ethics*, 295.

3. O'Connor and Franklin, "Free Will," Sec. 2.2.

though every incompatibilist holds, as the name implies, that free will and such determinism are incompatible, not every incompatibilist believes that free will actually exists. For incompatibilists in fact divide into two radically different camps, one of which rejects the thesis of determinism itself and the other of which rejects the existence of free will altogether. Whereas the *libertarians*, as they came to be called,[4] argue that we humans have free will and that the thesis of determinism is therefore false, others in the incompatibilist camp, sometimes called *hard determinists*,[5] argue that the thesis of determinism is true and hence that no one in fact has free will. This dispute among incompatibilists is clearly an instance of what we have called a genuine disagreement over a matter of substance (see the introduction); it is not, in other words, a mere verbal dispute arising from two parties using the same term, "free will," in two different senses.

But what about the major dispute that will occupy a lot of our attention in this book: the dispute between libertarians and compatibilists? To what extent is that a disagreement over a genuine matter of substance and not a mere verbal dispute, as we have called it? If we set aside the issue of moral responsibility for the moment and focus our attention only on arguments concerning the nature of free will, it is hard to discern just where any real disagreements

4. It is important to distinguish a libertarian in this *philosophical* sense from a libertarian in the *political* sense, a proponent of limited government. For many libertarians in the latter sense have in fact been compatibilists.

5. The term "hard determinism," typically used in contrast to the term "soft determinism" (another term for compatibilism) is unfortunate insofar as it can conjure up misleading images in the minds of students—as if one billiard ball slamming into another might illustrate hard determinism whereas one gently nudging another might illustrate soft determinism.

might actually lie. As an illustration, Alvin Plantinga once expressed the view of many early libertarians this way: "If a person is free with respect to a given action, then he is free to perform that action and free to refrain from performing it; no antecedent conditions and/or causal laws determine that he will perform that action, or that he won't."[6] The basic idea here is that being free with respect to some action in a given set of circumstances requires that, whether one performs this action or refrains from it, one could have chosen to do otherwise in something more than the compatibilist's *conditional sense* explained above. It requires instead that one could have chosen to do otherwise in the following *categorical sense*: in the exact same circumstances in which one freely chose to do something at a time T, that is, without any event prior to T having been different, it was nonetheless within one's power to have chosen otherwise. Call this *the power of contrary choice*.

So do Plantinga and the compatibilists disagree over the issue of whether a fully deterministic universe might include a person's having the power to do what this person most wants to do in a given situation? Not at all. Do they perhaps disagree, then, over the issue of whether someone might have the power of contrary choice, as Plantinga understands it, in a fully deterministic universe? Of course not. In fact, they even agree concerning the implications of what Plantinga *calls* "free will." Here are several such implications. If a scrupulously honest banker should find it psychologically impossible, on account of some deeply held moral and religious convictions, to accept a bribe, then this banker could not refuse the bribe freely in Plantinga's libertarian sense. Similarly, if a young mother, filled with love for her newborn baby, should find the idea of torturing her baby to death utterly unthinkable, or should find

6. Plantinga, *God, Freedom, and Evil*, 29.

it psychologically impossible not to care for her baby in a given situation, then neither could she care for her baby freely in the sense that Plantinga has described. Or finally, if the perfected saints in heaven have no desire whatsoever to disobey God and indeed should find it psychologically impossible to do so (in part because they find the whole idea utterly stupid), then neither could they obey God freely in the relevant sense.

Because these are all validly drawn implications from the way in which Plantinga and some of the early libertarians have defined a technical use of the term "free will," some libertarians have concluded that only a small number of our actions are truly free in the relevant technical sense. C. A. Campbell (1897–1974) thus famously restricted free will in this sense to contexts "of moral temptation," that is, to contexts in which we experience a conflict between inclination or desire, on the one hand, and a sense of moral obligation, on the other. Similarly, without restricting free will to cases of moral temptation, Peter van Inwagen nonetheless concluded at one time "that one has precious little free will, that rarely, if ever, is anyone able to do otherwise than he in fact does."[7] Other libertarians, such as Timothy O'Connor, have roundly criticized such restrictivism.[8] But the important point in our present context is not how frequently, if ever, it is within our power to act differently than we in fact do act; the important point is how to assess those specific cases, such as our honest banker who refuses a bribe and our loving mother who cares for her baby, where acting otherwise would have been psychologically impossible in a given situation. Whereas many compatibilists would call these instances of someone acting freely, a few libertarians, though by no means all of them, would never cite them as

7. See van Inwagen, "When Is the Will Free?" 224–25.

8. See O'Connor, *Persons and Causes*, 102–3.

instances of someone acting freely. Any dispute over what to call such actions, however, would appear to be purely verbal insofar as it appears to arise because two parties have simply assigned different meanings to a technical use of the term "free will."

Beyond that, just as no compatibilist should treat the above conditional analysis as a *sufficient condition* of the power to act otherwise, neither should a libertarian treat the *categorical* analysis as a sufficient condition of acting freely. For suppose that a schizophrenic young man should kill his loving mother, believing her to be a sinister space alien who has devoured his real mother; and suppose further that he does so in a context in which he categorically could have chosen otherwise (in part, perhaps, because he worries about possible retaliation from other sinister space aliens). Why should such an irrational choice, even if not causally determined, be any more compatible with a genuine moral freedom than a rigorous determinism would be? Either our seriously deluded beliefs, particularly those with destructive consequences in our own lives, are in principle correctable by some degree of powerful evidence against them, or the choices that rest upon them are simply too irrational to qualify as free moral choices. So the moral here is that neither the compatibilist's conditional analysis nor the libertarian's categorical analysis of the power to act otherwise qualifies as a sufficient condition of acting freely, and both of them, furthermore, require essentially the same additional condition: the absence of certain kinds of irrationality, which is a point that we shall explore further in chapter 4 of this work.

SOME VARIETIES OF THE LIBERTARIAN VIEW

We have considered so far a form of the libertarian view that identifies free will with *the power of contrary choice*. According to that view, no fully determined choice, not even a choice determined by one's own character together with the details of a given situation, will qualify as a genuinely free choice. For a choice is truly free only when the one who makes this choice at a given time categorically could have chosen otherwise at that time. So call this the *simple libertarian view*.

A rather perplexing objection to this view can be adapted from Harry Frankfurt's influential 1969 article entitled "Alternate Possibilities and Moral Responsibility," wherein he sets forth what is commonly called, not surprisingly, "Frankfurt style counterexamples" to the so-called principle of alternative possibilities that the simple libertarian view identifies with free action. Suppose that after some deliberation I decide on my own to vote for candidate A in a given election. But suppose also that, unbeknownst to me, I could not have decided otherwise for the following kind of reason: some person with extraordinary powers or perhaps some device implanted in my brain would somehow have prevented the decision from going the other way. Because this external power over my decision-making process is designed so as never to be engaged in the event that I decide on my own to vote for candidate A, as by hypothesis I do, I remain morally responsible for that decision even though I would never have been permitted to have decided otherwise. Here the basic idea seems to be that I am allowed to decide on my own only if I make the decision that someone else prefers that I make, but I am somehow blocked from making the opposite decision *on my own*. For similar reasons, some might also claim that in such a case I *freely* vote for candidate A even though I could not have decided

13

otherwise; and I bring up such putative cases because the literature dealing with them is now as voluminous as the arguments concerning them have become exceedingly complicated.

But fortunately, we need not get into the weeds at this point because many libertarians have additional (and more straightforward) reasons for denying that acting freely always requires the power to act otherwise (as the principle of alternative possibilities would require). Many libertarians thus concede to the compatibilist that an appropriately formed character can indeed determine a genuinely free choice in the proper circumstances. Here the idea seems to be that an agent's character is appropriately formed only when the agent is at least partly responsible for it. Robert Kane thus speaks of certain "voluntary 'self-creating' or 'self-forming' actions (including refrainings) in the life histories of agents for which the agents are personally responsible."[9] These self-forming actions, says Kane, are "both undetermined . . . and such that the agents willingly performed them and 'could have voluntarily (or willingly) done otherwise' . . . ."[10] Although undetermined—and, as some might say, self-generated or self-originated—they are also *self-forming* in the sense that they help to determine or shape the agent's present motives, purposes, and character traits: "Agents with free will . . . must be such that they could have done otherwise on some occasions of their life histories with respect to some character- or motive-forming acts by which they make themselves into the kinds of persons they are."[11] In a similar vein, Laura Ekstrom has likewise suggested that our judgment that an action is praiseworthy "may presuppose the idea that the agent's good character is

9. *Significance of Free Will*, 75.

10. Kane, *Significance of Free Will*, 75.

11. Kane, *Significance of Free Will*, 72.

ultimately of his own making . . . ."[12] And finally, James F. Sennett defends the free will of the saints in heaven by in effect arguing that they have freely chosen their own moral character. "A character that is libertarian freely chosen," he therefore suggests, "is the only kind of character that can determine compatibilist free choices."[13] Call this, for want of a better descriptive phrase, the *integrated libertarian view*.

Here it is important, I believe, to distinguish between two subtly different claims: (1) the claim that a person's character is appropriately formed only when that person's life history includes some undetermined choices that could have gone the other way; and (2) the claim that a person's character is appropriately formed only when that person is in some way (that no one has yet clearly explained) responsible for it. The second claim in particular raises some exceedingly difficult and confusing questions concerning the concept of *moral responsibility*. Is it true, for example, that being morally responsible for one's own actions requires that one be self-created, or *causally* responsible for the person one now is, or causally responsible for one's own character? For my own part, I see no reason why this should be true at all. What such moral responsibility requires instead, as we shall see, is that one be rational enough to learn important lessons from the consequences of one's own actions.

In any case, a more recent form of the libertarian view seeks to drive a wedge between two closely related, but by no means identical, claims that libertarians have commonly made: (a) the claim that a free action requires alternative possibilities, if not always at the time of choosing freely, then at some prior time in a person's life history, and (b) the claim that acting freely requires a person to be the sole

12. Ekstrom, *Free Will*, 165.

13. Sennett, "Freedom in Heaven?" 74.

and ultimate source of the relevant action. As one proponent of this position, Eleonore Stump, has put it, "Someone who rejects compatibilism can maintain that it is possible for an agent to act with free will, indeterministically, [even] when he could not have done otherwise."[14] She does not deny that acting with free will is often *accompanied* by a power to act otherwise. But her reflection on the Frankfurt-style counterexamples to the principle of alternative possibilities seems to have led her to deny that the power to act otherwise is essential to the very nature of free agency. What really is essential, she thinks, is that the agent's "own intellect and will are the sole ultimate source or first cause of her act."[15] Like the alternative possibilities requirement, this sourcehood requirement could never be met in a fully deterministic universe. For if determinism were true, then our own intellect and will could never be "the sole ultimate source or first cause" of actions whose causes lie in the distant past long before we were even born. So call this the *source libertarian view*.

One virtue of Stump's explanation, as I see it, is her explicit reference to the intellect and, by extension, to one's capacity for sound reasoning, for drawing reasonable inferences from experience, and for holding reasonable beliefs concerning the best course of action (see chapter 4 for more on these points). But if free will does indeed require indeterminism, as Stump insists it does, then how on earth, one might ask, could the reality of indeterminism fail to include alternative possibilities *of some kind or another*? Does it not follow from the very nature of indeterminism that more than one outcome from a set of initial conditions is causally possible? Granted, we can easily imagine cases where an alternative is blocked even as someone nonetheless acts

14. Stump, "Augustine and Free Will," 126.
15. Stump, "Augustine and Free Will," 126.

freely—as when, for instance, someone installs a mecha-
nism in my car that, when activated as I approach an intersection, prevents the car from turning right. If I should
freely turn left at this intersection, then this would clearly
be a case where I could not have done otherwise in the
sense that I could not have freely turned the car to the right.
Alternative possibilities nonetheless remain in such a case
insofar as I still might have freely chosen to turn right and
might have even *tried* (unsuccessfully) to do so. For reasons
of this kind, some who favor a sourcehood account of free
will acknowledge that such an account cannot eliminate
altogether alternative possibilities of every kind. According
to David Hunt, however, an omniscient God with an infallible foreknowledge of the future would effectively block
every alternative possibility without interfering with human freedom. It would block every alternative possibility,
he suggests, "because no one can falsify the foreknowledge
of an infallibly omniscient being"; and this would not interfere with human freedom because the sourcehood account
of that freedom would remain intact.[16]

Although the integrated libertarian view, as I have described it above, could perhaps accommodate some forms
of the source libertarian view, it could not accommodate

16. Hunt explains his understanding of these matters in a couple
of short videos, which are available, respectively, at the following
two URLs: https://www.closertotruth.com/series/has-god-settled-
the-future#video-48187; https://www.closertotruth.com/series/
how-could-god-know-the-future#video-48188. In the first video
above, Hunt claims that "no one can falsify the beliefs of an infallibly
omniscient being." And in the second video, he claims that we do
not perform an act because God infallibly foreknew that we would
do that; instead, God foreknew that we would do this because that
is precisely what we do in the future. But if the second claim is true,
as I believe it is, then it is hard to see why the power to do otherwise
would constitute a power to falsify the foreknowledge of an infallibly
omniscient being. See chapter 6 for more on this topic.

the view of Hunt and others that libertarian freedom could exist apart from any alternative possibilities at all. So for that reason, among others, I am here treating the source libertarian view as a distinct view with issues of its own.

A FINAL THOUGHT

In the following chapter, we'll examine an important argument—the so-called Consequence Argument—for the conclusion that free will is incompatible with determinism, and then in chapter 3 we'll examine an equally important argument for the conclusion that free will is incompatible with indeterminism. But of course, if these two arguments are both sound, then it would appear as if the concept of *free will* is simply incoherent; and that very conundrum has led Peter van Inwagen to declare that free will remains a mystery at the present time. According to van Inwagen:

> Since the publication of *An Essay on Free Will*, it has become increasingly clear to me that free will is a philosophical mystery—something that philosophers do not understand at all. . . . I do not mean to imply that free will is a mystery in the theological sense: something that is beyond all possibility of human comprehension. That may or may not be the case. I contend only that as of this date, no philosopher has achieved an understanding of free will. That may be because free will is indeed something that human beings are incapable of understanding, but it may be because we human beings have not yet discovered the right way to think about free will.[17]

It seems to me, even as it does to van Inwagen, that "we human beings have not yet discovered the right way

17. Van Inwagen, "Thoughts on *Free Will*," 20.

to think about free will"; in particular, the perennial temptation among libertarian philosophers to identify free will with a categorical power to act otherwise has led them, I believe, down a blind alley. To begin with, it has led more than a few of them to reject some paradigm cases of what we would ordinarily count as the freest of all actions, such as our aforementioned loving mother whose motherly instincts make it psychologically impossible for her not to care for her baby. Accordingly, the right way to think about free will should enable us, in my opinion, to accept such paradigms of acting freely without, at the same time, embracing compatibilism, and I want eventually to propose an analysis aimed at achieving that goal. As I see it, moreover, we must locate the mystery of free will squarely in the midst of an even greater mystery: that of creation itself. But don't take this to be a theological claim. For by "creation" in the present context, I have in mind nothing more nor less than the origin of creatures like you and me, creatures capable of conscious experience, moral reasoning, and purposive actions. Whether we humans are the product of a long process of blind evolution, a long process of divinely assisted evolution, or the direct creation of God at some point in the past, the origin of creatures like us remains, I believe, a deep and unfathomable mystery.

As for the apparent incoherence in the very concept of *free will*, I want eventually to suggest a way out of this particular quagmire. The main problem with libertarian accounts, especially those offered by Christian philosophers who address the question of our ultimate destiny, is that no one seems to have provided a sufficiently complete account. Too many feel content merely to provide a necessary condition or two of acting freely, and some simply inform us that someone acts freely in the libertarian sense only if that person's actions are not causally determined by factors outside of his or her control. But if, in the spirit of van Inwagen, one wants to solve the mystery of free will and to discover an illuminating way to think about it, I suggest that one should try to formulate a non-trivial sufficient condition of it, a sufficient condition that obviously *can* be satisfied. If that sufficient condition is not also a necessary condition, it may not apply to all cases of free action, but it should provide a starting point for a proper understanding of it. In chapter 4, therefore, I shall offer what I take to be a sufficient condition of acting freely and offer some additional suggestions for what the role of indeterminism (understood as random chance) plays in the life of a morally responsible free agent.

The following schematic, although no substitute for the more detailed summaries of the various positions outlined in this chapter, includes some brief reminders concerning them.

Thesis of Determinism The thesis that every event has a sufficient cause and therefore no event is undetermined	**Compatibilism** Free will is compatible with the thesis of determinism.		
	Incompatibilism Free will is incompatible with the thesis of determinism	**Hard Determinism** Because the thesis of determinism is true and is incompatible with free will, free will does not exist	
Denial of the Thesis of Determinism		**Libertarianism** Because free will is a genuine reality and is incompatible with determinism, the thesis of determinism is false.	**Simple Libertarian View** One performs an act freely only when it is also within one's power to have refrained from that action.
			Integrated Libertarian View Insofar as our own undetermined choices shape our own character, that character can determine additional free choices.
			Source Libertarian View Identifies the essence of freedom with sourcehood and de-emphasizes the importance of alternative possibilities.

DISCUSSION QUESTIONS ON CHAPTER (1)

(1) Based on our preliminary survey, are you inclined to believe that free will could indeed exist in a fully deterministic universe? If so, why? If not, which view do you find to be the more plausible: the view that every event has a sufficient cause and hence that there is no such thing as free will, or the view that there is genuine free will and hence that the thesis of determinism is quite false? Explain your answer.

(2) Again, based on our preliminary survey, does it seem plausible to you that moral freedom should *always* require a psychological possibility of acting otherwise? If our loving mother, for example, should find it psychologically impossible to neglect her beloved baby, does it follow that her caring for her baby is not a free act? If so, would it somehow enhance her moral freedom if she were able to do something unthinkable such as to torture her baby to death?

(3) If you argue that free will is incompatible with both determinism and indeterminism, then you appear to be arguing that the concept of free will is blatantly incoherent. But there also appears to be no mystery about such incoherence: it signifies nothing that actually exists. So do you agree that the concept of free will is blatantly incoherent? If so, then do you reject this concept altogether? If not, then how might you defend the idea of its coherence?

2

THE CONSEQUENCE
ARGUMENT AGAINST
COMPATIBILISM

PERHAPS THE MOST INFLUENTIAL contemporary argument
against compatibilism is sometimes called, for reasons that
should become apparent shortly, the Consequence Argument; and this argument rests upon two crucial premises:
first, that we now have no control over the state of the universe at any chosen time in the remote past, and second,
that none of us who exist as creatures in the universe has
any control over the laws of nature that govern how the universe operates. But granting the truth of these two premises,
how does the argument proceed from there? According to
Kevin Timpe in a fine book on free will, "The Consequence
Argument is based upon a fundamental distinction between the past and the future. . . . [It] builds upon this view
of the fixed nature of the past to argue that if determinism is
true, the future is not open in the way" that common sense

believes it to be; that is, what will happen in the future appears to be no less unavoidable than what has already happened in the past.[1] In his own classic discussion of the argument, Peter van Inwagen likewise sought to capture its basic intuition with the following preliminary statement:

> If determinism is true, then our acts are the consequences of the laws of nature and events in the remote past. But it is not up to us what went on before we were born, and neither is it up to us what the laws of nature are. Therefore, the consequences of these things (including our present acts) are not up to us.[2]

About this argument van Inwagen also suggests that it is "obvious"—not in the sense that "it's obviously right," but in the sense that it "should occur pretty quickly to any philosopher who asked himself what arguments could be found to support incompatibilism."[3] And when he used the term "consequences" in the first sentence of the above quotation, he evidently had in mind the *logical consequences* of determinism; as Timothy O'Connor once commented, "If these two factors together [the laws of nature and the state of the universe at some time in the remote past] *entail* all of my future decisions, then those 'decisions' aren't really up to me."[4] Not surprisingly, therefore, much of the contemporary discussion of this argument focusses on the question of whether the *unavoidability* of both the laws of nature and the past will transfer through entailment to our present decisions and actions, making these unavoidable as well.

1. See Timpe, *Free Will*, 26–27.

2. Van Inwagen, *Essay on Free Will*, 16.

3. Van Inwagen, *Essay on Free Will*, 16.

4. O'Connor, *Persons and Causes*, 4—my italics.

AN INITIAL DIFFICULTY

In order for *unavoidability of a relevant kind* to transfer through entailment, you must have, first of all, a genuine case of entailment. But as we saw in chapter 1, there is more than one way in which the thesis of determinism could be true. Take the total state of the universe in the year 1000 BC. Why suppose that, given the truth of determinism, the state of the universe in 1000 BC together with the laws of nature would entail anything whatsoever about me? Suppose, just for purposes of illustration, that the birth of Christ was fully determined by God but not fully explicable in terms of the laws of nature plus some set of antecedent conditions that existed back in 1000 BC. Had that one event not occurred, the entire future course of history would presumably have been vastly different from what has actually occurred since the year 1000 BC; indeed, for all I know, I might never even have been born. As defended by someone like Jonathan Edwards, then, the thesis of determinism carries no implication that the conjunction of the laws of nature and the state of the universe at any point in the remote past entails the entire future course of our earthly lives. That would, after all, eliminate altogether certain kinds of providential control by God. Theological determinists thus typically deny that the created order is itself a self-contained deterministic system, and they deny this in part because, as they see it, God directly causes many specific events to occur within the created order, not all of which are recognized as miracles. God may even encounter some people directly during their lifetimes, such as we read in the story of Moses speaking with God through the burning bush or in the story of St.. Paul speaking with the risen Lord on the road to Damascus; such experiences as these, if they literally happened, presumably could not be fully explained in terms of ordinary laws of nature. So the thesis of determinism does not even entail that every action of every person can be traced to a set of causal conditions that existed within the universe before that person was born; much less could they be traced to a set of conditions that existed sometime in the remote past.

But isn't all of this beside the point? If every event that occurs within the universe is causally determined, does it really matter for free will whether some of these events are directly determined by some divine action and are therefore not explicable in terms of the laws of nature? Well, it certainly matters to the validity of van Inwagen's specific argument against compatibilism, whether or not it matters to the soundness of some other argument against compatibilism. So let us now examine more closely what is, perhaps, the least controversial claim that the Consequence Argument makes: the claim that no one, not even God, *now* has any control over the state of the universe at some time in the remote past. Few people, whether they be compatibilists or incompatibilists on the question of free will, would likely challenge that claim. It is thus common to speak of a unique kind of necessity—sometimes called "accidental necessity"—brought about by the mere passage of time. But we also have compelling reasons to believe, so I shall argue in the following section, that in the very nature of the case the unique necessity or uncontrollability of the past cannot transfer to the future through entailment. For even if a set of past events or conditions should causally determine some future action and thus render its nonoccurrence causally impossible, this would not transfer to the future the unique uncontrollability that is characteristic of the past.

THE NECESSITY OF THE PAST: JUST HOW SHOULD WE UNDERSTAND IT?

So what is it, exactly, that makes deliberation about the past seem so utterly pointless? We can regret the past or perhaps even glory in it, but we cannot normally deliberate about it because there is nothing, so it appears, that we can now make happen in it; it is simply too late for that. Still, the expression "necessity of the past" is something of a misnomer.[5] For it is not, strictly speaking, the *necessity* of the past, but its *inaccessibility* to us—the fact that our actions normally have no effects in the past—that prevents our having any choice at the present time about the shape of the past. Just as you and I can have no direct effect on what is now happening in a galaxy far, far away, neither can we now affect the past unless some of our actions should somehow have effects in the past. As Linda Zagzebski has put it, "So the necessity of the past may simply be the principle that past events are outside the class of causable events. There is a temporal asymmetry in causability because everything causable is in the future."[6] And as Kevin Timpe comments, "Given the direction of the flow of time *and the normal*

5. In a brilliant, although (as I see it) easily misunderstood and too often neglected, article with the intriguing title "Is the Past Unpreventable?" George Mavrodes argues in effect that there is no such thing as the so-called necessity of the past. For being past does not by itself render anything necessary. It is certainly true that, for any event *e* and time *t*—and here it matters not whether *t* is now in the past, the present, or the future—someone's knowing that *e* occurs at *t* entails that no one ever has or ever will prevent (or obviate) the occurrence of *e* at *t*. But just as knowing that *e* occurs at *t* does *not* entail that no one could have prevented this occurrence prior to the time of its occurrence, neither does it entail, he argues, that no one could still have the power (unexercised, of course) to prevent (or obviate) this occurrence at a time later than *t*.

6. Zagzebski, "Foreknowledge and Free Will," sec. 2.6.

direction of causation [my emphasis], it seems as if the future is open in a way that the past is not."[7]

But suppose now that some of our actions did have effects in the past. Timpe imagines such a scenario when he claims, correctly, that not even someone traveling backward in time, assuming for a moment that this should be possible, could "literally change the past." He then goes on to argue: "So, at most, the possibility of time travel allows for agents to have causal impact on the past, not for agents to change what has already become the past. The past thus appears to be fixed and unalterable."[8] The problem with this way of putting the matter, however, is that the future may appear to be no different from the past in a similar manner. For just as "the possibility of time travel allows for agents to have causal impact on the past," so the normal direction of causation enables our actions to have a causal impact on the future; and just as the possibility of time travel would not allow "for agents to change what has already become the past" into something else, neither does the normal direction of causation allow our actions to change what will in fact become the future into something else. And this may make it look as if the future is no less fixed and unalterable than the past. Still, what we all can do, insofar as our free actions have effects in the future, is to change the future from *what it would have been had we acted differently* into what it will in fact be; and similarly, a time traveler whose free actions did have effects in the past might change the past from what it would have been had the time traveler acted differently to what it actually was.

Here, then, is the precise sense in which, according to common sense, the past, unlike the future, is fixed and unalterable: we sometimes have an *unexercised* power over

7. Timpe, *Free Will*, 26.
8. Timpe, *Free Will*, 26–27.

the future that we do not normally have over the past. That is, we sometimes have an unexercised power to alter the future from what it will in fact be to *what it would be should we act otherwise than we in fact choose to act*. But this power is always unexercised because what we actually do—the power we in fact exercise—is what determines the shape of the future. So the most critical issue, to repeat the point, nonetheless concerns the direction of causation. More than a few hold that backward causation (including someone traveling into the past) is metaphysically impossible; and without trying to resolve that particular issue, I shall simply presume that, given the laws of nature as they are, effects do not precede their causes in time. And if that is true, it also explains why, in the very nature of the case, the necessity of the past—that is, its unique inaccessibility—cannot transfer to the future. For our actions unquestionably do have effects in the future; hence, insofar as we have some control over our own actions, it is always possible to have some control over the future of a kind that we do not [normally] have over the past.

Lest I be misunderstood here, in no way am I denying the principle that what follows logically from a fixed and unalterable fact about the past is itself a fixed and unalterable fact—albeit a fixed and unalterable fact *about the past*. My point is that too many fail to distinguish carefully enough between the necessity (or the inaccessibility) of the past, on the one hand, and some unrelated forms of necessity, on the other. The necessity of the past is, in the first place, very different from an absolute logical or metaphysical necessity, which by its very nature is independent of time. It is also very different from causal necessity. For consider a causally determined event, such as the sun's rising over Salem, Oregon, tomorrow morning. Would not some fixed and unalterable fact about the past, such as the fact that the universe was in a certain state yesterday plus the fact that certain laws of nature govern the movements of the sun and various planetary bodies, entail this fact about tomorrow morning? Not at all. For if we assume the existence of a supreme Creator of the universe, then this Creator, at least, would continue to have the power, however unexercised it may be, over the motions of the sun and various planetary bodies. He would continue to have the power, in other words, to cause the earth to stop spinning in relation to the sun even as he keeps everything else in balance, and that would be the power to make something like the story in Joshua 10:12–14 to become literally true. My point here, as should be obvious without further elaboration, is not that anyone should take this story literally. For however one takes this Old Testament story—whether one takes it as an ancient fable, a confused description of a solar eclipse, or an accurate historical account—no theist should deny that the Creator has such power or even the logical possibility of his exercising it between now and tomorrow morning. If he chooses not to exercise such power and not to suspend the relevant laws of motion, then it may indeed be causally determined that the sun will rise tomorrow. But again, that has nothing to do with transferring the inaccessibility (or the so-called necessity) of the past to the future and everything to do with ordinary causal necessity—which, I must continue to insist, should not be confused with the inaccessibility of the past.

Similarly, even if it should be causally determined, apart from divine interference, that a man will die from a fatal illness at midnight tonight, this man may still have the power to get out of bed tomorrow morning. He may have the power to do something such that, were he to do it, a prior miracle would have occurred; he may even have the power to do something that would help to bring about this prior miracle. For if "prayer changes things," as many religious people believe, then his own prayers and those of his family and friends may even contribute to God's decision to perform such a miracle. Once again, we are talking here about logical possibilities rather than what is likely to occur. But if such miraculous events do not occur because God does not exercise his power to perform them, then the sun's rising tomorrow morning and the man's dying tonight at midnight will indeed be causally determined. Still, that has nothing to do, once again, with transferring the inaccessibility (or the so-called necessity) of the past to the future and everything to do with ordinary causal necessity—which, I must continue to insist, should not be confused with the fact that the past is inaccessible to us in a way that the future is not. We are thus left with the simple intuition, which I share, that the thesis of determinism is incompatible with anyone ever acting freely, and our question in the present context is whether the Consequence Argument provides any substantial support, which I doubt it does, for that basic intuition.

THE SUM OF THE MATTER

Conclusive proofs are hard to come by in philosophy, if they are possible at all outside the context of formal logic and mathematics. And even though I personally agree, as I have already indicated, with the view that moral freedom could never exist in a fully deterministic universe, I nonetheless believe that the Consequence Argument itself has at least two weaknesses, one more serious than the other.

We have already discussed the less serious weakness: the false assumption that, if determinism is true, it *follows* that the laws of nature plus an antecedent set of conditions can explain the occurrence of every event in the universe.

So let us now simply assume that, contrary to the opinion of Jonathan Edwards and other theological determinists, our universe is indeed a self-contained causal system in the sense that from well before the dawn of human history its entire future has been a consequence of these two factors: the laws of nature and the total state of the universe at any time in the remote past. The Consequence Argument proposes, correctly, that I have no control over the laws of nature and no control over the state of the universe at any time in the remote past. It then points out that, if the universe is itself a self-contained deterministic system in the sense just defined, then all of my future actions are a consequence of these two factors over which I have no control, and it concludes that I therefore have no *real* control over any of my own future actions either.

But herein lies a more serious weakness—namely, that the conclusion of the Consequence Argument appears to be an invalid inference. Or at least so a compatibilist will argue. For consider again a point made in the previous section concerning the direction of causation and a fundamental asymmetry between the past and the future. If our actions have effects in the future but no effects in the past, especially in the remote past, then the following kind of argument seems obviously invalid:

> I now have no choice of any kind, determined or otherwise, concerning the shape of the past and no choice, determined or otherwise, concerning how the laws of nature operate; if the relevant determinism is true, therefore, then I have no choice of any kind, not even a determined one, concerning what to eat for breakfast tomorrow.

Such an argument, to repeat the point, seems not only invalid, but *obviously* invalid. Similarly, just as you cannot validly deduce that our actions have no effects in the future from the premise that they have no effects in the past and no effect upon how the laws of nature operate, neither can you validly deduce, so a compatibilist will argue, that we have no control *of any kind* over our future actions from the premise that we have no control of any kind over the past and the laws of nature. So if these inferences are all invalid, the door seems to be open for a compatibilist to specify a sense of "ability" such that we have no ability of a relevant kind to control the past or the laws of nature and yet have an ability of the relevant kind, perhaps even a kind sufficient for moral responsibility, to control our future actions. And perhaps the best known example of such an analysis includes the early compatibilist's so-called conditional analysis of the ability to act otherwise, already discussed in chapter 1. As we saw there, this conditional analysis cannot stand alone as "a *sufficient condition* of someone's having the power to act otherwise in the compatibilist sense"; and more to our present point, perhaps, neither will it qualify as a sufficient condition of someone's having an ability to control one's future actions. Writing in defense of compatibilism, Tomis Kapitan thus acknowledges that the "traditional conditional analyses have been rightly repudiated, for they fail to supply a sufficient condition for ability."[9]

But so what? Both compatibilists and incompatibilists can agree, I presume, that newborn babies do not acquire a morally significant freedom and do not become morally responsible for their actions until they have crossed a minimal threshold of rationality (more on that in chapter 4); and even after they become adults, any irrational fears that result in compulsions or obsessions of a psychiatric kind can clearly interfere with their ability to act freely and to choose otherwise in particular cases. So why cannot a compatibilist simply claim the following concerning any

9. Kapitan, "Reply to the Consequence Argument," 136.

adult who has the good fortune of remaining free from such irrational fears, compulsions, and obsessions? Such a person has the power to act otherwise on a given occasion provided that *this person* (the one who is free from psychiatric illness) would have acted otherwise had he or she chosen (or undertaken) to do so. Even if one should object that this would not be a legitimate case of a power to act otherwise, moreover, a compatibilist could simply reject the idea, even as some libertarians do, that our power over our future actions always requires a power to act otherwise in the first place.

So is my point here that a satisfactory compatibilist account of human freedom is indeed possible? Not at all. Personally, I am skeptical of the idea that creatures like you and me—that is, independent centers of consciousness and reason—could even exist in a self-contained deterministic system. My point instead is that no one should find it surprising when someone who does not already share my conviction that a self-contained deterministic universe would be incompatible with moral freedom finds the Consequence Argument less than persuasive. Neither should anyone find it surprising that a compatibilist account of our unexercised power to act otherwise (such a power, remember, is always unexercised) carries the following implication: one would exercise one's power to act otherwise in a self-contained deterministic universe only if some aspect of the past or some law of nature had been different. A compatibilist is, after all, a compatibilist! As Tomis Kapitan once commented, "Naturally, those who have not yet ruled out compatibilism will hardly be persuaded by an argument that begins by placing an indeterministic condition on ability."[10] If from the outset we do place "an indeterministic condition on ability," then we have already assumed the point at issue between

10. Kapitan, "Master Argument for Incompatibilism?" 132.

compatibilists and incompatibilists; and if we do not place such a condition on ability, then we have no reason to suppose that the precise sense in which the past and the laws of nature are inaccessible to us would transfer to the future.

CONCLUSION

The debate over the Consequence Argument has not only been contentious at times; it has also featured some highly formalized and technical arguments over matters of detail. My own strategy in this chapter, therefore, has been to stick to the "big picture," so to speak, and to explain why in the very nature of the case the Consequence Argument is unlikely to persuade someone who is not already persuaded of its conclusion. And furthermore, most philosophers on both sides of this debate agree that the two sides have come to a kind of philosophical impasse. Timothy O'Connor, himself a strong proponent of this argument, thus seems unable to disguise his disappointment when he writes: "I have already acknowledged that such a response as I have given to the compatibilists' position will not move the firmly persuaded, though it seems to me no less correct and decisive for all that."[11] Similarly, Daniel Speak, who also finds the Consequence Argument plausible and persuasive, agrees that the philosophical community as a whole has reached a kind of stalemate (or impasse) over it.

> Still, in the debate between compatibilists and incompatibilists, we remain at a philosophical impasse, with neither party being much moved by the challenges of the other. Furthermore, if philosophical history is any guide, it is unlikely that the impasse will be circumvented by *one more move* in the ongoing dialectic, whether

11. O'Connor, *Persons and Causes*, 17.

the move is made by either the proponent or the opponent of the Consequent Argument.[12]

Given such a philosophical impasse, Speak makes the suggestion that philosophers might do well to turn their "attention more directly to the deeper *meta-philosophical values* (if such there be) that ground the competing positions in the debate over the Consequence Argument."[13] According to Richard Double, a meta-philosophy is "a view of what philosophy is, what philosophy can do, and, especially, what philosophy is *for*;[14] and Speak seems to have in mind something similar. For our purposes, it should suffice to think in terms of a broader set of prior convictions, whether they be religious, secular, or otherwise philosophical, that may heavily influence the various positions we take on the issue of free will and determinism. In my own case, for example, one contributing reason for why I am not a compatibilist has little or nothing to do with my understanding of moral responsibility; it stems instead from my belief that God created the universe with the intention of producing independent centers of consciousness, that is, rational agents distinct from himself, who are capable of learning on their own valuable lessons from experience and from the consequences of their own actions. But if God fully determines, either directly or indirectly through secondary causes, every event that occurs in his creation, then only one agent capable of independent action would seem to exist, namely God himself. Accordingly, God can create dependent beings capable of independent action, so it seems to me, only in a context in which he does not in general determine their individual choices.

12. Speak, "The Consequence Argument Revisited," 128.
13. Speak, "The Consequence Argument Revisited," 128.
14. Double, *Metaphilosophy and Free Will*, 4.

Now consider, by way of contrast, the beliefs of Daniel Dennett, an important contemporary philosopher committed to both atheism and compatibilism. His atheism makes it perfectly natural for him, first, to distinguish *mere determinism* from various *non-coercive forms of control*, and then to argue as follows: however exhaustively the past may determine our future, "the past does not control us" in the same way a purposive agent might do so. That's because "there is nothing in the past to foresee and plan for our particular acts"; neither are there "feedback signals from the present to the past for the past to exploit."[15] Remarkably, Dennett even concedes that a Laplacean "superhuman intelligence" that also determines the future could easily control us and would indeed undermine our compatibilist autonomy.[16] As even Dennett appears to concede, therefore, not even compatibilist autonomy could exist in a theistic universe in which God plans for and likewise causally determines every event that occurs.

DISCUSSION QUESTIONS ON CHAPTER 2

(1) Perhaps the most important claim made in this chapter is that the so-called necessity of the past—its inaccessibility, that is—cannot transfer to the future through entailment. That claim is relevant not only to the Consequence Argument, but also to certain arguments for fatalism (see chapter 5) as well as the argument that divine foreknowledge is incompatible with human freedom (see chapter 6). Do you find this crucial claim persuasive? If so, why? If not, why not?

(2) Another important claim made in this chapter is that the following is a logical consequence of theological

15. Dennett, *Elbow Room*, 72.
16. Dennett, *Elbow Room*, 61.

determinism: only one agent capable of independent action would in fact exist, namely God himself. Do you agree with that? If not, why not? If so, do you believe that created persons would be morally responsible for their actions nonetheless? Explain your answer.

(3) Consider the claim, "Conclusive proofs are hard to come by in philosophy." That claim raises the further question, "Just what is a proof anyway?" According to normal usage, an argument is valid if its conclusion follows logically from its premises and it is sound if it meets two conditions: (a) it is valid, and (b) its premises are all true. So presumably a proof must be sound as well as valid. But is that enough to constitute a proof? Of course not. For suppose that God in fact does exist and created the universe. If so, then the following might very well be a sound argument: *If God created the universe, then God exists; God created the universe; therefore, God exists.* But that would hardly qualify as a conclusive proof of God's existence. So what conditions other than soundness, in your opinion, must a conclusive proof of something meet?

3

INDETERMINISM AND
RANDOM CHANCE

EVEN AS LIBERTARIANS ARGUE that *determinism* is incompatible with free will, so many compatibilists have argued that *indeterminism* is incompatible with free will; and even as many libertarians have employed the Consequence Argument as a favorite argument for their position, so many compatibilists have employed an argument concerning random chance as a favorite argument for their position. According to the latter argument, any degree of indeterminism in the process of making a decision introduces an element of random chance into it, and any degree of random chance in this context is incompatible with perfect freedom and moral responsibility.

Now, as first mentioned back in chapter 1, some philosophers have defended the claim that, as a necessary condition of moral responsibility, free will is incompatible with both determinism and indeterminism; and these philosophers have thus concluded that the concept of free will is simply incoherent. As we have also seen, Peter van Inwagen appears to defend both incompatibilities even as he continues to believe in free will. He thus concludes not that the concept of free will is blatantly incoherent, but instead that free will remains "a philosophical mystery—something that philosophers do not understand at all." Before we can explore that issue any farther, however, we must first examine more fully the argument that any degree of indeterminism in the process of decision making implies some degree of random chance, which is itself incompatible with acting freely.

A FAULTY ARGUMENT

Here is how Moritz Schlick once expressed the standard compatibilist argument concerning chance:

> We can speak of motives only in a causal context; thus it becomes clear how very much the concept of responsibility rests upon that of causation, that is, upon the regularity of volitional decisions. In fact if we should conceive of a decision as utterly without any cause (this would in all strictness be the indeterministic presupposition) then the act would be entirely a matter of *chance*, for chance is identical with the absence of cause; there is no other opposite of causality. Could we under such conditions make the agent responsible? Certainly not.[1]

These remarks include the following three-step argument:

(1) If a decision D of mine occurs "utterly without any cause," then D is "entirely a matter of *chance*."

---

1. Schlick, *Problems of Ethics*, 156.

(2) If D is entirely a matter of chance, then I am not responsible for D.

(3) Therefore, if D occurs utterly without any cause, then I am not responsible for D.

But this argument seems defective in several ways. In the first place, just what might it mean to say that some decision occurs "utterly without any cause"? Are we to imagine here a decision that has no necessary causal conditions at all and no causal influences of any kind? Or, are we to imagine instead a decision that is not entirely the product of sufficient causes that lie outside the agent's control? Beyond such questions as these, some libertarians, though by no means all of them, defend the idea of agent causation, according to which agents or persons, understood as substances rather than merely a collection of states and events, can cause a decision or some other action, even though no prior events are sufficient causes of their doing so. Richard Taylor once described an agent or a person, therefore, as "a self-moving being" and went on to write: "For on this view it is a person, and not merely some part of him or something within him, that is the cause of his own activity."[2] This idea of a substance, as opposed to another event or set of events, causing some event is no doubt controversial. But my point here is merely that the expression "utterly without any cause" is far too imprecise to be of any use in the present context.

Consider next the expression "entirely a matter of chance." Suppose that you are a high school teacher weighing the pros and cons of reporting a certain student to the high school principal; suppose further that it is not fully determined which considerations on either side of the issue happen to occur to you during your period of deliberation;

2. Taylor, *Metaphysics*, 51.

and suppose finally that, had one of these considerations not occurred to you (by chance, if you will), you would not have decided it best to report this student to the principal. Would you say that your decision was *entirely* a matter of chance? That might seem to imply that your decision was made for no reason at all, which is absurd, or that it was made unintentionally and without any purpose of your own, which is equally absurd. For whatever decision you make in such a context, this decision will not be entirely a matter of chance in the sense of having been made for no reason and no purpose at all. Are we to conclude, then, that if your decision is not *fully* determined by conditions that already existed prior to your deliberation, then it was at least *partly* a matter of chance?

One could, of course, guarantee the truth of the first premise above simply by making it true by definition. That may be what Schlick was up to when he tells us that "chance is identical with the absence of cause; there is no other opposite of causality." But given at least one ordinary use of the term "chance," a chance occurrence is simply an unanticipated, unexpected, and unplanned for event, and such an event may very well be causally determined. When a man seeks shelter under a tree at the very instant that a bolt of lightning strikes the tree and seriously injures him, we have no reason to deny that this particular unforeseen occurrence (the lightning striking the tree at just this moment) was the product of sufficient causes. So in that sense, a chance occurrence hardly qualifies as the "opposite of causality." We are all free, of course, to define (or even to redefine) our terms in any way we please, so long as we make our definitions clear. If by "utterly without any cause" Schlick simply means "not causally determined" and by "chance" he also means "not causally determined," then his first premise would be equivalent to the following redundancy:

>   (1*) If a decision D of mine is not causally determined, then D is not causally determined.

And even though that premise is true enough, it is also utterly trivial and uninformative. Worse yet, the second premise of the above argument would be equivalent to

>   (2*) If D is not causally determined, then I am not responsible for D.

And (2*) assumes as a premise the very thing Schlick is trying to establish as a conclusion—a question-begging premise, if ever there was one. So it looks as if Schlick's argument breaks down altogether.

THE REAL PROBLEM OF RANDOM CHANCE

As we saw back in chapter 1, not all libertarians hold that we choose freely only when we categorically could have chosen otherwise. But those who hold the integrated libertarian view, as we called it there, do hold that we choose freely today only if at various times in our life history we could have chosen otherwise than we in fact did choose at those specific times. Such libertarians as Robert Kane, Laura Ekstrom, and James F. Sennett thus hold that, in a case where a fully formed character determines a choice, one makes that choice freely only if one has some kind of ultimate responsibility for one's own character, and one meets that condition, according to these libertarians, only if one's past choices include some that genuinely could have gone the other way.

Let us consider more closely, then, a case where someone makes a choice in a context where that person categorically could have chosen otherwise. Having such a power surely requires something more than an infinitesimally small probability of choosing otherwise: the kind of thing that certain interpretations of quantum mechanics imply might exist even in cases of ordinary causation on the macro level. For as Michael Almeida and Mark Bernstein point out, "There is a well-known interpretation of quantum mechanics according to which any ordinary situation involves some small probability that an extremely strange event occurs. If you drop a plate, for instance, there is a small chance that the particles composing the plate fly off sideways and the plate will not hit the floor . . . ."[3] But such an infinitesimally small chance as that, so small that we cannot even point to a single instance of something like that actually happening, will hardly suffice for a genuine (or a robust) power to act otherwise. At the very least, therefore, the power to act otherwise in the relevant categorical sense must include a *realistic* chance, as I shall here call it, of it actually happening. Such an idea is no doubt incurably vague. But concerning the infinitesimally small chance of a dropped plate not hitting the ground in a context where, given the laws of nature, that would be the normally expected result, suffice it to say that this would fall well below the threshold of a realistic chance of something actually occurring.

But why hold that a genuine (or a robust) power to choose otherwise in a particular context implies that whichever way one chooses the result will be, at least partly, a matter of random chance? Suppose that yesterday I had a non-decisive reason R to do A and a non-decisive reason R* to refrain from A, and suppose that, after deliberating for a while, I made the choice, uncaused by any prior events, to do A in a context in which a choice to refrain from A

3. Almeida and Bernstein, "Rollbacks, Endorsements, and Indeterminism," 488.

was likewise causally possible. If this is a context, as some libertarians would have it, in which I categorically could have chosen otherwise, it seems fair to ask how one might distinguish such a choice from a random selection between alternatives. For what other than random chance might "explain" why I acted from R and chose to do A when I categorically could have acted from R* and could have chosen to refrain from A? Granted, whichever choice I had made, whether I had chosen to do A or had chosen to refrain from A, would have been distinguishable from chance in the sense that I, the agent, would have acted for a reason. But what nonetheless remains unexplained, whether properly so or not, is why I should have acted from R and have chosen to do A when I categorically could have acted from R* and have chosen to refrain from A; in that respect, it is hard to see why my having chosen to do A rather than having chosen to refrain from A was not the product of random chance or at least the product of random elements in some decision making process. Nor do I see how one can remove the apparent arbitrariness here simply by calling this an instance of agent causation, which does nothing to remove the mystery.

It is not even clear, by the way, that compatibilists and libertarians must disagree here on some matter of substance. For as the libertarian *extraordinaire*, Robert Kane, has himself admitted:

> But can we not at least say that, if indeterminism is involved, then *which* option is chosen is "arbitrary"? I grant that there is a sense in which this is true. An ultimate arbitrariness remains in all SFAs [self-forming actions] because there cannot in principle be sufficient or overriding *prior* reasons for making one set of reasons prevail over the other. But I argue that

such arbitrariness relative to prior reasons tells us something important about free will. It tells us, as I have elsewhere expressed it, that every undetermined self-forming choice (SFA) "is the initiation of a 'value experiment' whose justification lies in the *future* and is not fully explained by the *past*. . . . [W]e say in effect, "Let's try this. It is not required by my past, but is consistent with my past and is one branching pathway my life could now meaningfully take. I am willing to take responsibility for it one way or the other"[4]

Personally, I am suspicious of the idea of self-forming actions. Although I do not deny that we can be morally responsible for our *actions*, I seriously doubt that we have some sort of ultimate responsibility for our own character. The problem, as Manuel Vargas once noted, is that "even freely chosen features of our lives and ourselves can, because of our epistemic limitations, yield *unanticipated* consequences."[5] One person may lie and cheat in pursuit of wealth and fame, only to discover that the result is emptiness and misery; and the circumstances surrounding this discovery may causally determine (even compel) a life-transformation. Another may sincerely cultivate moral integrity and inadvertently produce some of the worst character traits: moral rigidity, self-righteousness, and a lack of compassion. As Bernard Williams once observed, "One's history as an agent is a web in which anything that is the product of the will is surrounded and held up and partly formed by things that are not" products of the will.[6] Indeed, the assumption that even God could consider how people exercise their libertarian freedom and, on that basis

4. Kane, "Responsibility, Luck, and Chance," 176.

5. Vargas, "The Trouble with Tracing," 282.

6. Williams, "Moral Luck," 29.

alone, divide them into the good and the bad, or into those who deserve a reward and those who deserve punishment, now seems to me radically confused.

But we can permit all of that to pass for now. The important point for our present purposes is Kane's concession that an "ultimate arbitrariness remains in all undetermined" actions performed in a context where the agent categorically could have chosen otherwise, and the reason for this is that "there cannot in principle be sufficient or overriding *prior* reasons for making one set of reasons prevail over the other." So in that respect, Kane seems to agree with the compatibilist that such a choice would include an element of random chance or, as he puts it, an element of arbitrariness.

PETER VAN INWAGEN'S ROLLBACK ARGUMENT

In support of the thesis that indeterminism in the process of decision making must include an element of random chance, Peter van Inwagen asks us to imagine that a woman named Alice decides whether to tell the truth or to lie on some important matter where, whichever choice she makes, she categorically could have chosen otherwise. We are also to imagine that she finally decides to tell the truth. But then van Inwagen asks us to "suppose that immediately after Alice told the truth, God caused the universe to revert to precisely its state one minute before Alice told the truth . . . and then let things 'go forward again.' What would have happened," he asks, "the second time?"[7] Perhaps the same thing would have happened, or perhaps the second time she would have lied. Finally, van Inwagen asks us to make two suppositions: first, "that God *a thousand times* caused the universe to revert to the state it was in" exactly one minute

7. Van Inwagen, "Free Will Remains a Mystery," 171.

before Alice decides whether to tell the truth or to lie, and second, "that we are somehow suitably placed, metaphysically speaking, to observe the whole sequence of 'replays.' . . . What should we expect to observe?"[8] He concludes that in all probability we would observe that "sometimes Alice would have lied and sometimes she would have told the truth"; and if the "replays" should continue indefinitely, a reasonably fixed percentage of lies and instances of truth telling should eventually emerge. Given a sufficient number of replays, therefore, we should get a pretty clear sense of the role that random chance plays in Alice's specific process of deliberation.

It is an intriguing thought experiment, one that illustrates nicely the point that Robert Kane and I both make in the previous section concerning the power to choose otherwise. But after making his point about random chance, van Inwagen then asks how anyone can claim that Alice acted freely: "If she was faced with telling the truth and lying, and it was a mere matter of chance which of these things she did, how can we say that—*and this is essential to the act's being free* [my emphasis]—she was *able* to tell the truth and *able* to lie?"[9] The assumption here is that the power to act otherwise comprises the essence of moral freedom, which is the very assumption that the Rollback Argument challenges. Interestingly enough, van Inwagen also makes the following confession at this point: "I confess I believe there is something wrong with this argument."[10] But he also notes that he cannot say what this is and perhaps also doubts whether anyone else has identified anything wrong with the argument.

---

8. Van Inwagen, "Free Will Remains a Mystery," 172.

9. Van Inwagen, "Free Will Remains a Mystery," 173.

10. Van Inwagen, "Free Will Remains a Mystery," 175.

An initial philosophical difficulty with the Rollback Argument, though perhaps not fatal to it as a *thought experiment*, arises for anyone who takes seriously the necessity of the past, as discussed previously in chapter 2. For the whole idea of God's reverting the universe back to a time just prior to when a given choice has already been made seems to express a metaphysical impossibility—namely, that of obliterating a past occurrence or something that has already happened in the past. So even if God wanted to do something like that, which is itself impossible, he still could not actually do it—unless, of course, God himself has power over the past and there is therefore no such thing as the necessity of the past.

Another problem, according to Michael Almeida and Mark Bernstein, is that the "Rollback Argument ignores the fact that chance is time dependent" and that "objective probabilities . . . change over time."[11] That "chance is time dependent" seems clear enough. If one minute prior to the time at which Alice tells the truth there was a 50/50 chance of her arriving at that decision, there may have been a 99 percent chance of her telling the truth an instant or two prior to her actually telling the truth. We can also imagine that, as sometimes happens in such cases, Alice deliberates for several days before the deadline finally arrives when she cannot avoid making a decision; and we might imagine further that, during this period of deliberation and struggle, she goes back and forth several times, sometimes coming close to deciding one way and other times coming close to deciding the other way, as different considerations occur to her. Prior to her finally making up her mind, moreover, Alice may have no idea, contrary to what Almeida and Bernstein seem to suggest, what her final decision will be; she

11. Almeida and Bernstein, "Rollbacks, Endorsements, and Indeterminism," 487.

has, after all, not yet made up her mind. But whatever her decision-making process *as a whole* might be like, the following seems indisputable: if this is to be a case where Alice could have decided otherwise in the libertarian's categorical sense, then there must be something more than an infinitesimally small probability of the process *as a whole* coming out differently. There must be a reasonably robust chance, as we have already indicated, that Alice might have decided to lie. And that is what gives point, it seems to me, to van Inwagen's type of thought experiment.

Almeida and Bernstein have nonetheless made an important point about endorsement: how rational agents often endorse their own actions. But do they not overstate the case when they write the following? "In almost every case of deliberate action we will find agents prepared to endorse their actions, endorse their endorsement and so on upward."[12] For though rational agents typically do continue *evaluating* their own actions, endorsement is only part of their evaluation; they just as often regret their deliberate actions, believe that they acted wrongly, and reassess their reasons for acting as they did. They also learn important lessons from the consequences of their own actions and especially from their mistakes, as they come to understand them. This process of evaluation is indeed essential to our moral freedom, I believe, but a categorical power to act otherwise would nonetheless require a kind of indeterminism on the macro level that surely does imply a degree of random chance or arbitrariness, as even Robert Kane has acknowledged.

We thus return to the problem described at the beginning of this chapter. If you believe, as I and other incompatibilists do, that free will could never exist in a

12. Almeida and Bernstein, "Rollbacks, Endorsements, and Indeterminism," 492.

fully deterministic universe; and if you also believe, as I and many compatibilists do, that indeterminism always includes an element of random chance, are you not then in danger of transforming the concept of moral freedom into a blatantly incoherent concept? That is the question we shall continue to explore in the following chapter.

DISCUSSION QUESTIONS ON CHAPTER 3

(1) Consider again the following claim made in chapter 2: "Conclusive proofs are hard to come by in philosophy, if they are possible at all outside the context of formal logic and mathematics." Are there ways, then, in which Moritz Schlick's Chance Argument or Peter van Inwagen's Rollback Argument, both of which are discussed in the present chapter, illustrate the truth of this claim about conclusive proofs? If so, why? If not, do you believe that one or both of these arguments would qualify as a proof? Explain your answer.

(2) According to Manuel Vargas, "even freely chosen features of our lives and ourselves can, because of our epistemic limitations, yield *unanticipated* consequences" for our character. If that is true, then how could it also be true that we have some kind of ultimate responsibility for our own moral character?

(3) Michael Almeida and Mark Bernstein point out that, according to "a well-known interpretation of quantum mechanics, . . . any ordinary situation involves some small probability that an extremely strange event occurs. If you drop a plate, for instance, there is a small chance that the particles composing the plate fly off sideways and the plate will not hit the floor." Do you agree with the claim made in this chapter that "such an infinitesimally small probability as that, so small that

we cannot even point to a single instance of something like that actually happening, will hardly suffice for a genuine (or a robust) power to act otherwise"? And if, alternatively, freedom requires a genuinely robust power to act otherwise, how might one distinguish such a power, if at all, from random chance? Explain your answer.

4

RATIONALITY AND THE NATURE OF MORAL FREEDOM

I HAVE ALREADY NOTED that libertarians and compatibilists can surely agree that moral freedom requires a minimal degree of rationality; and for that reason alone, those in both camps would no doubt exclude lower animals, small children, the severely brain damaged, the seriously demented, and perhaps even paranoid schizophrenics from the class of free moral agents. Some libertarians and compatibilists may have serious disagreements over the question of whether the relevant rationality could exist in a self-contained deterministic universe, as I have called it. But I cannot imagine anyone in either camp rejecting the idea that moral freedom requires that one has surpassed a certain threshold of rationality.

So just how should we understand the relevant threshold here? It must surely include an ability to reflect upon and to evaluate one's own actions, to draw inferences with some degree of accuracy from one's own experience and from the consequences of one's actions, and to learn important lessons, as the evidence continues to pile up, concerning the conditions of one's own happiness. Above all, it must include an ability to make reasonable judgments, however fallible they may be, concerning the best course of action in a given situation. But as with borderline cases in general, it is probably impossible to say exactly when a maturing child, let us say, becomes rational enough to advance above the relevant threshold or when someone suffering from age-related dementia sinks below that threshold. In the case of a woman suffering from Alzheimer's Disease, for example, there need be no exact instant at which her ever-diminishing rationality removes the last shred of her remaining freedom; it is enough that at some point she has clearly lost the ability to make reasonable judgments concerning the best course of action and has therefore lost the ability to act freely.

THE ISSUE OF COHERENCE AGAIN

We thus return to Peter van Inwagen's contention that "free will is a philosophical mystery—something that philosophers do not understand at all." Because I agree with him that, in general, "we human beings have not yet discovered the right way to think about free will," it is important, as we have already noted, to distinguish a mystery in this sense from sheer incoherence. For if, given a specific concept of it, free will is, without any qualification at all, incompatible with both determinism and indeterminism, then that concept is simply incoherent; there is no mystery about that, and the claim that we have free will in that incoherent sense is simply false. So the trick, I take it, is to explain the very different roles that indeterminism and determinism could play in the life of a free moral agent and to do so in a way that avoids a blatant inconsistency at this point.

Now the best way to avoid such an inconsistency requires, I believe, that we come to appreciate two points: first, that freedom and moral responsibility, no less than rationality itself, are typically matters of degree, and second, that some of the very conditions essential to our *emergence* as independent rational beings and therefore as free moral agents—conditions that include various degrees of indeterminism—are themselves obstacles to *full* freedom and moral responsibility. The basic idea here is that our emergence as independent rational creatures, capable of acting on our own, requires a causal break from the past, even as the very indeterminism responsible for such a causal break can also introduce an element of irrationality into our behavior. And that irrationality can sometimes be an obstacle to full freedom and moral responsibility.

But why suppose that the emergence of an independently rational creature, capable of acting on its own, requires a causal break from the past in the first place? One general answer concerns what some have called "the autonomy of reason," which is the idea that reason must proceed in accordance with its own self-determined principles and canons. As Warner Wick once put it, "all talk of truth . . . would be utterly *pointless* if there were nothing to it but causal influences that induced me to say or think *this*, while causing you to opine *that*";[1] or, as C. S. Lewis once put it, "rational thought is not part of the system of Nature. Within each man there must be an area (however small) of activity which is outside or independent of her. In relation to Nature, rational thought goes on 'of its own accord' or exists 'on its own.'"[2]

1. Wick, "Truth's Debt to Freedom," 535. The italics are Wick's.
2. Lewis, *Miracles*, 27.

Because not everyone, I suspect, will likely find persuasive the Lewis claim in particular, it may help at this point to examine separately each of the two different ways, discussed earlier, in which someone might imagine the thesis of determinism being true. Whereas a theological determinist, such as Jonathan Edwards, held that, as our Creator, God himself causally determines, either directly or indirectly through secondary causes, every event that occurs in his creation, some non-theists seem to have held that our universe, being both uncreated and self-contained, is nonetheless fully deterministic in the sense that every event occurring in it—subsequent to the "Big Bang," at least—has a sufficient cause. Now, according to Michael Almeida and Mark Bernstein, "The best science informs us that we likely inhabit an indeterminist world" (or an indeterminist universe);[3] and if they are right about this, as I suspect they are, then neither of these deterministic conceptions of our universe is accurate. But that is not our present concern. For whether or not we do live in a deterministic universe, the issue before us now concerns the *logical possibility* of an independent rationality somehow emerging in such a universe.

Accordingly, in what follows we shall consider first the example of theological determinism. For whether or not anything like a traditional God in fact exists, the assumption that such a God both exists and causally determines every event that occurs in our universe illustrates two points very nicely: why free will requires a causal break of some kind from the past as well as from eternity itself and why the indeterminism that makes such a causal break possible is also an obstacle to full freedom and moral responsibility. Then, after considering some related matters, I'll make a

3. Almeida and Bernstein, "Rollbacks, Indorsements, and Indeterminism," 384.

final suggestion at the end of this chapter concerning the idea of a self-contained and fully deterministic universe, as some non-theists have imagined our universe to be.

INDETERMINISM AND MORAL FREEDOM

Consider more closely now the kind of theological determinism that we find in someone like Jonathan Edwards. Back in chapter 2, you may recall, I expressed my own conviction that "if God fully determines, either directly or indirectly through secondary causes, every event that occurs in his creation, then only one agent capable of independent action would seem to exist, namely God himself." It also seems to follow that only one independently rational being, capable of reasoning on its own, would exist as well. Or, to put it another way, neither any human being nor any other created individual would qualify as an independently rational creature. For suppose that God should causally determine every one of our thoughts (whatever it might be), every inference we might draw (whether it be drawn accurately or mistakenly), and every evaluation we might make of some body of evidence (however rational or irrational that evaluation might be). Under such conditions as these, it is hard to know what it would even mean to say that we are somehow reasoning *on our own*. It also seems plausible to say that a creature qualifies as being *independently rational* only if no other rational mind controls that creature's reasoning process in the absolute way just described. And as we saw back in chapter 2, it looks as if even Daniel Dennett, despite his overall commitment to compatibilism (albeit in an atheistic universe), would agree with such a claim as that.

Consider next some of the complications that even an omnipotent Creator might face in a context where indeterminism has an essential role to play in his creative purposes. Suppose, by way of illustration, that God intended to create a *collection* of independently rational creatures who are (a) aware of themselves as distinct from their environment and from other people, (b) capable of acting *on their own* and of making reasonable (albeit highly fallible) judgments concerning the best course of action in a variety of different situations, and (c) capable of learning important lessons from experience and from the consequences of their own actions. What might a Creator's options have been in creating such independently rational creatures as these?

The assumption behind this question is that not even omnipotence could create such independently rational creatures without meeting certain broadly logical or metaphysically necessary conditions of their *coming into being*. So if, as I have suggested, one of these metaphysically necessary conditions is a severance from God's direct causal control; and if God also wanted these minimally rational creatures to learn valuable lessons from experience and from their interactions with each other, then perhaps God would have had no choice but *to permit their embryonic minds to emerge and to begin functioning on their own in a context of ambiguity, ignorance, and indeterminism.* Even the story of Adam and Eve in the Garden of Eden illustrates the point nicely. For, according to the account in Genesis, our first parents, like every other child, first emerged and became conscious of their surroundings without knowing anything at all about the distinction between good and evil. Neither, therefore, did they know anything of substance about the nature of God. Yes, they knew that some authority figure, sort of like our earthly parents whom we first encounter even before we are fully aware of our surroundings, had commanded them not to eat the fruit from the tree in the middle of the garden. But like the children they were in all but size, they had no clear understanding of why the command was issued in the first place, or why it would be a good thing for them to obey it. So in this story, at least, Adam and Eve first emerged and began making choices, it seems, in a context of ambiguity, ignorance, and misperception.

As a further illustration of the point, consider simple ignorance and the view of many theistic philosophers that our freedom in relation to God requires that we start out in a context in which he remains hidden from us. If we were to begin our earthly lives with a full and complete knowledge of God and, in particular, with a clear understanding that he is the ultimate source of human happiness, this knowledge would not be a personal discovery at all. It would not be acquired through a complex learning process in which we formulate hypotheses, test them in our own experience, and then learn for ourselves over time important lessons about life and the nature of God. But consider also how relative degrees of ignorance can severely restrict our freedom and, in that sense, can become an obstacle to a fully realized freedom. If I am ignorant of the fact that someone has laced the local water supply with LSD, then I have not freely chosen to ingest the LSD, however freely I may have chosen to drink the water. And similarly for the free-will theist's understanding of divine hiddenness: insofar as the ambiguities, the ignorance, and the misperceptions in a given set of circumstances conceal God from us, or at least make unbelief a reasonable option, they also make committing ourselves to God in these circumstances more like a blind leap in the dark than a free choice for which we are morally responsible. So if anything, God's hiddenness can render us less, rather than more, responsible for our failure to love the one whose true nature and very existence remain hidden from us.

Now even as, according to some theistic philosophers, our freedom in relation to God requires that we first emerge as rational agents without a full and complete knowledge of God, so it also requires that we first emerge in a context in which our actions are not fully determined. For if, as many theistic libertarians would acknowledge, a created free agent could never be a mere extension of the physical universe and a free choice could never be the product of sufficient causes that lie outside the choosing agent's control, then a context of indeterminism must surely be, at the very least, a necessary condition of someone's *emergence* as a free moral agent. It also seems to me utterly unlikely that all of our present actions are fully determined, however determined some of them might be by more immediate beliefs and desires. For we all *in fact* emerge and begin making choices in a context of ambiguity, ignorance, and misperception, where indeterminism could easily play a huge role in the choices (or quasi-choices) we make, in providing the necessary causal break from the past, and in allowing us to emerge as independent agents who interact with our environment, learn from experience, and make discoveries on our own. So once again, the trick is to distinguish between the role that indeterminism plays in our *emergence* as free moral agents and the role it continues to play *after* we have become sufficiently rational to learn important moral lessons from the consequences of our undetermined choices.

Put it this way: it is essential to our moral freedom that we *begin* making moral choices in a context where these choices are not fully determined by sufficient causes; for if they were so determined, they would most likely be fully determined by conditions external to the emerging agent. But it is also essential to our moral freedom that we should be rational enough to learn from our mistakes. So once we begin learning some relevant moral lessons—from our misguided or bad choices in particular—some of our freest actions may be those voluntary actions where, given our own reasonable judgment concerning the best course of action, the alternative is no longer psychologically possible for us. *Some of our freest actions, in other words, may occur in a context in which we are unable to choose otherwise*—especially in cases where the alternative seems utterly unthinkable or irrational.

MORAL FREEDOM AND THE POWER TO ACT OTHERWISE

Now consider again some of our ordinary paradigms of free action, as I have called them, such as the loving mother who cares for her newborn baby and the honest banker who refuses a bribe. As we saw back in chapter 1, some libertarians reject these so-called paradigms in cases where a mother's love makes it psychologically impossible for her to abandon her baby or where a banker's deeply held moral and religious convictions make it psychologically impossible for him to accept a bribe; other libertarians are prepared to accept such paradigms, provided that our loving mother and honest banker somehow have a kind of ultimate responsibility for their own moral character, which is the very thing that makes acting otherwise psychologically impossible for them on a given occasion.

But toward the end of chapter 3, I also expressed my own skepticism about the idea that we are personally responsible for our own character—in part because, whatever control we might have over what we do in specific situations, we have virtually no control over the long-term effects that our actions have on our own moral character.

Many libertarians seem to adopt, as a kind of unexamined metaphysical assumption, the idea that a good moral character is typically a product of good moral choices even as a bad moral character is typically a product of bad moral choices. Robert Kane seems to adopt just such an assumption when he paints the following picture:

> The probabilities for strong- or weak-willed behavior are often the results of agents' own past choices and actions, as Aristotle and other thinkers have insisted. Agents can be responsible for building their moral characters over time by their (moral or prudential) choices or actions, and the character building will be reflected by changes in the probabilities for strong- or weak-willed behavior in future situations. Each time the [alcoholic] engineer resists taking a drink in difficult circumstances, he may strengthen his will to resist in the future; and conversely, when he succumbs, his will to resist may lessen (or crumble altogether, as sometimes happens with alcoholics).[4]

But even if such a picture reflects accurately *some* of our experience in *some* contexts—very limited ones, I believe—the way in which the free choices in someone's life history, assuming there are such, affect one's present character and motives may be just the opposite of what Kane has imagined; worse yet, the effect is apt to depend upon intervening factors utterly outside the agent's control.

Kane is right, of course, about the alcoholic engineer, at least partly. One biochemical effect of alcohol on the brain, at least in the case of alcoholics, seems to be that it undermines the will to resist another drink. But that is not even close to the whole story. For as an alcoholic friend of

4. Kane, *The Significance of Free Will*, 180.

mine once pointed out, the longer she stayed off the alcohol, the easier it became during times of stress to deceive herself into believing that this time a couple of drinks would do no harm; so curiously, the longer she resisted the temptation, the stronger her temptation became. Indeed, it was not until she had succumbed to temptation and had binged terribly on a good many occasions that she finally learned to recognize such deception for what it was. So in that sense, her experience was just the opposite of what Kane describes: the more often she successfully resisted temptation, the harder it became to resist such temptation in the future; and the more often she succumbed to it and experienced the destructive consequences of doing so, the easier it became to resist such temptation in the future.

So here is an obvious case where some bad choices helped to undermine a bad (or at least a weak) moral character. Experience also provides examples where freely resisting temptation, particularly in difficult situations, seems to weaken the will over time rather than to strengthen it. I dare say that many men—and this would include some Christian ministers I know—have sincerely (even fervently) resisted sexual temptation for many years, only to succumb to it, finally, in middle age. For it may happen that the harder a man tries, for the most earnest of reasons, to suppress his childish yearnings and unrealistic fantasies, the more intense his temptations become and the more likely he is to succumb to them in an explosion of destructive behavior. Perhaps it would be misleading, however, to describe this as a case where some good choices help to undermine a good character. For if we suppose that the described behavior really is destructive and really is the product of childish yearnings and unrealistic fantasies, then it is also, perhaps, the product of deeper character flaws of which the agent is unaware—character flaws that first need to be exposed before they can be dealt with effectively.

It seems to me, in any case, that no one has yet provided a coherent account of what it might even mean to say, in the words of Laura Ekstrom quoted previously, that "the agent's good character is ultimately of his own making." Are not the most virtuous among us typically the last to credit themselves and the first to credit good fortune—or perhaps the grace of God, if they are religious—for their own moral virtues? Are they not wise enough not to attribute their moral virtues, whatever these might be, to the virtuous nature of certain free choices buried in their causal history? Nor should it come as any surprise that the Christian religion, particularly as we encounter it in the letters of St.. Paul, has always presented a good character as a gift from God rather than as a product of a created agent's own making. Paul even hints in the eleventh chapter of Romans that our disobedient acts may sometimes be especially useful to God in producing a good character through correction. For why else would he assert that God shuts all of us up to our disobedience as an expression of his mercy to us? (Rom 11:32). In fact, the Pauline perspective seems to be that a bad moral character differs from a good one in just this respect. Like alcoholism and drug addiction, a bad moral character will inevitably enslave a person in one of two ways: either it will undermine over time one's power to follow one's own judgment concerning the best course of action, or it will eventually undermine altogether one's ability to learn from experience and to make reasonable judgments concerning the best course of action. I contend that this is just what makes a bad moral character *objectively* bad: it will tend to undermine over time one's rational control over one's own actions. But a good moral character is just the opposite. For whereas a bad character leaves the will in bondage to something destructive and therefore evil (Christians call it sin), a good character inevitably expands one's rational control over one's actions and in that sense liberates the will. That, at least, seems to have been Paul's view of the matter, and he therefore spoke of salvation as if it were a release from bondage, a means by which our very *wills* are set "free from the law of sin and death" (Rom 8:2).

Accordingly, the Pauline perspective on freedom and the will seems to imply that a free will—that is, a will no longer in bondage to "the law of sin and death"—does not always require the power to choose otherwise, particularly when such a choice would be utterly irrational; it requires instead an ability to assess one's actions with some degree of rationality and to appreciate the evidence that arises concerning the conditions of one's own happiness. In that respect at least, the Pauline perspective seems to accord very well with Susan Wolf's Reason View, which she has set forth in her book *Freedom within Reason*. She writes:

> According to the Reason View, . . . responsibility [as well as the freedom that responsibility requires] depends on the ability to act in accordance with the True and the Good. If one is psychologically determined to do the right thing for the right reasons, this is compatible with having the requisite ability. . . . But if one is psychologically determined to do the wrong thing, for whatever reason, this seems to constitute a denial of that ability. For if one *has* to do the wrong thing, then one *cannot* do the right, and so one lacks the ability to act in accordance with the True and the Good.[5]

A couple of clarifications are perhaps in order here. First, when Wolf speaks of someone being "psychologically

5. Wolf, *Freedom within Reason*, 79.

determined" to do something, I interpret this to mean that someone's own desires, beliefs, evaluations, and the like determine one's choice or action on a given occasion; it need not mean that one's choice or action is the product of sufficient causes that lie either in the distant past or in eternity itself. And second, in the same context Wolf goes on to write: "The Reason View is thus committed to the curious claim that being psychologically determined to perform good actions is compatible with deserving praise for them, but that being psychologically determined to perform bad actions is not compatible with deserving blame."[6] Setting aside the issue of praise and blame for a moment, the relevant asymmetry for moral freedom is just this: whereas *freely* doing something one believes to be morally wrong or prudentially bad requires the power to act otherwise, *freely* doing something one believes to be the right thing to do does *not* always require the power to act otherwise. For in cases where acting otherwise seems, for the best of reasons, utterly unthinkable or irrational, moral freedom in the sense of having a rational control over one's own actions does not require the power to act in a way that seems to be utterly irrational and thus contrary to one's own best interest.

As for the issue of moral responsibility and that of deserving either praise or blame, such issues are a bit more complicated. For even when some tragic event is unavoidable in the moment—as, for instance, when a drunk driver has no power in the moment to avoid killing a pedestrian—one might still be responsible for having put oneself into such a situation. So, to avoid this and other complications, I have here restricted myself to an asymmetry thesis concerning the nature of moral freedom. If one finds it psychologically impossible to do what one judges to be the

6. Wolf, *Freedom within Reason*, 79.

best thing to do in a given situation, then one's will is in a kind of bondage analogous to what an alcoholic or a drug addict might experience. But if, by way of contrast, our loving mother and honest banker should find it psychologically impossible to violate their own conception of the right thing to do, this may simply be because their wills are free from such bondage as an alcoholic or a drug addict might experience.

A PROPOSED SUFFICIENT CONDITION OF MORAL FREEDOM

So perhaps we are now in a position to set forth a sufficient condition of moral freedom. According to Wolf's suggestion in the above quotation, the relevant freedom "depends on the ability to act in accordance with the True and the Good"; it depends, that is, on the ability "to do the right thing for the right reasons." But even as her view is more subtly nuanced than these remarks may at first appear,[7] so I will here tweak her remarks a bit and speak of an ability to act in accordance with one's own reasonable judgment concerning the best course of action. By a "reasonable judgment" in the present context, I do not mean a *correct* judgment and certainly not a correct *moral* judgment. For even as adults, we humans continue to live and to make highly fallible judgments in a context marked by various degrees of ambiguity, ignorance, and even illusion. Or, as St.. Paul once put it, "For now we see through a glass, darkly" (1 Cor 13:12—KJV). And one of the most persistent (and pernicious) of our human illusions is, I would suggest, the belief that we can benefit ourselves over the long term at the expense of others. In any case, the reasonableness of a

7. See, for example, chapter 6 of *Freedom within Reason*, a chapter entitled "The True and the Good."

mistaken judgment concerning the best course of action will depend, at least in part, on the extent to which this judgment is in principle correctable, that is, the extent to which one is willing to accept additional evidence against it. Alternatively, the more resistant one is to powerful evidence against it, the more unreasonable that judgment ultimately is.

So herein lies my proposed sufficient condition of moral freedom. Independently rational agents, assuming they have passed a minimal threshold of rationality and that they are thus capable of reflecting upon and evaluating their own actions intelligently, are in a position to act freely whenever two conditions are met:

> (a) they have made a reasonable (and hence correctable) judgment concerning which of the actions available to them in a given context is, all things considered, the best course of action to take in that context, and

> (b) they have the power to follow their own judgment in this matter, whether or not they in fact do follow it.

Because this proposed sufficient condition of moral freedom is not also intended as a necessary condition, it carries no implication, I should perhaps point out, that moral freedom always requires some judgment concerning what would be the best course of action in a given context; much less does it imply that there must always be exactly one best course of action in any context in which one acts freely.

But just what does it mean to say that an action is *available* to some person in a given context? Perhaps the best way to understand this concept is in contrast to that of an *alternative possibility*, as some libertarian philosophers have understood it. When these philosophers speak of alternative possibilities—as in "the principle of alternative possibilities"—they are not speaking of mere logical possibilities; they are instead speaking of alternative actions within a given person's ability or power to perform. But the concept of an *available action*, as I here understand it, includes many actions that are psychologically impossible for an agent actually to perform. Recall the traditional compatibilist's conditional analysis of the expression "could have done otherwise." Although such an analysis seems utterly inadequate as a sufficient condition of someone's having the power to act otherwise, it fits perfectly with the idea of an action being available to someone in my sense. After all, however psychologically impossible it would be for our loving mother to torture her beloved baby to death, she has the physical capability and the know-how to do such a horrendous thing; that is, she would successfully accomplish such an action if, as is not even psychologically possible for her, she should undertake to do it. So in that sense, torturing her beloved baby to death, unlike flying like a bird, remains one of her available actions.

Reflecting on the issue of rationality thus provides us with both a necessary condition and a sufficient condition of the freedom that moral responsibility requires. An obvious *necessary condition* of the relevant freedom is *a minimal degree of rationality*, including an ability to deliberate about, to reflect upon, and to evaluate one's own actions intelligently; and a *sufficient condition* of it, I have now suggested, is *having the power to follow one's own reasonable judgment concerning which of the available actions in a given situation represents the best thing to do in that situation*.

But at this point an important question arises. If one should accept the above sufficient condition of acting freely, would it not follow, at the very least, that human freedom would be logically possible within a self-contained and fully deterministic universe? For even if, as we have seen, theological determinism of a kind that includes God's absolute causal control over every human thought and every human judgment seems clearly incompatible with an independent human rationality, Daniel Dennett's atheism enables him to argue, as we have also seen, that "there is nothing in the past to foresee and plan for our particular acts" and neither are there "feedback signals from the present to the past for the past to exploit." And that may seem to leave open the logical possibility, at least, that the above sufficient condition of acting freely could indeed be met in a deterministic universe that exists independently of any theistic God who created it, intelligently designed it, or directly causes various events to occur within it. Because such a universe would be *both* self-contained *and* fully deterministic, it follows that we live in such a universe only if all of our own psychological states at any given time are a logical consequence of the two factors already discussed in connection with the Consequence Argument against compatibilism: namely, conditions that already existed in the remote past and the laws of nature. So the only question left in the present context is whether the relevant rationality could exist (or emerge) under such conditions as these.

It seems likely, however, that the dispute over this latter question might result in a philosophical impasse similar to what we encountered in connection with the Consequence Argument. For just as many libertarians will argue that a blind determinism would be no less incompatible with independent human rationality than an all-controlling divine mind would be, so many compatibilists will continue to believe that the libertarian argument rests upon a confusion of some kind or another. So in response to such an anticipated impasse, I would offer the following suggestion. If libertarians and compatibilists can at least agree concerning the role that rationality must play in the life of a free moral agent and can agree, in particular, that some level of irrationality is incompatible with acting freely, then they can perhaps set aside any lingering theoretical disagreement over whether reliable reasoning could in fact exist in a self-contained and fully deterministic universe. For suppose that two scientists should strongly disagree on the issue of whether human rationality—that is, a human mind that reasons properly—would be possible in a self-contained and fully deterministic universe (absent any intelligent design of our cognitive faculties); these scientists might nonetheless agree on the scientific merits of many scientific theories. Similarly, two philosophers who disagree on the issue of whether a reasoning mind could ever emerge in a fully deterministic universe might nonetheless come to agree on the role that human rationality must play in human freedom. So perhaps we can simply let the proverbial chips fall where they may on the issue of whether the relevant rationality would be metaphysically possible in a fully deterministic universe—particularly if, in fact, we live in an indeterministic universe, as Michael Almeida and Mark Bernstein insist we do.

SOME CONCLUDING REMARKS

The essence of freedom, I have suggested in this chapter, is *the ability to follow the dictates of one's own reasoning powers, provided that one has passed the relevant threshold of rationality.* In no way, then, does freedom of belief require an ability to believe just anything one might fancy believing, however irrational or contrary to the available evidence such a belief might be. We see this most clearly, no doubt, in the case of a simple empirical belief, such as the belief that fire can burn and cause terrible pain. With respect to such a belief as that, freedom of belief hardly requires an ability to reject the *compelling evidence* most of us have concerning the nature of fire. By "compelling evidence" here I mean (roughly) evidence that both *justifies* a belief and removes one's power on some occasion to reject the belief in question. What freedom of belief requires instead is independent rational judgment and a minimal ability to follow the evidence where it properly leads. Neither does freedom of choice in the case of our loving mother require that she have the power to reject those settled convictions and values that compel her to continue protecting her beloved baby from harm as far as she can. What her freedom requires instead is an ability to follow her own judgment concerning the best course of action in the matter of caring for her baby.[8]

Now certainly many of our moral and religious beliefs are a lot more complicated and a lot more subject to error than simple empirical beliefs, such as our normal beliefs about the properties and dangers of fire. So insofar as we humans continue to "see through a glass, darkly," it is hardly surprising that different cultural backgrounds and different

8. Unlike a mother cat whose instincts fully determine that she will feed her newborn kittens, most human mothers, in addition to having similar biological instincts, have also surpassed the relevant threshold of rationality that is required, in my opinion, for them to qualify as a free moral agent. Unlike a cat, in other words, most human mothers at least have the capacity to reflect upon their own actions, however instinctive they may be, and to ask whether their actions are right or wrong. So even in a context in which a given mother's biological instincts seem to take over—in part because she sees no good reason to act contrary to them—she will make a reasonable judgment, however fallible it may be, that it is best to follow these instincts and to care for her children. I see no good reason to deny, therefore, that she acts freely in doing so.

experiences would result in different moral and religious perspectives. Neither is it surprising that different people would freely move in opposite directions, some from one religious perspective to another or even from theism of some kind to atheism, and others would freely move from atheism to theism. A first-rate and well-known philosopher thus explained to me several decades ago how he had moved "inch by inch" (his words) from a firm commitment to Christianity as a young man to atheism later in life, while others, such as C. S. Lewis, have explained how they moved inch by inch, so to speak, from atheism to theism.[9]

But here is a point concerning such diversity of thought not to be neglected. On the one hand, if the traditional God does not exist—if, that is, there does not exist a supremely perfect and supremely resourceful personal being who created and providentially controls our universe—then this diversity of inconsistent moral and religious perspectives seems unlikely ever to be resolved. On the other hand, however, if such a God does exist, as many theists from a variety of different traditions believe, such a divine being would be resourceful enough, it seems, to correct all of our mistaken judgments over an indefinitely long period of time and to do so without interfering with human freedom at all (see chapter 6 for more on this point). In short, given a proper understanding of the role that rationality must play in the life of a free moral agent, God could eventually correct all of his loved ones who have fallen into error; and he could do so simply by honoring their own free choices and allowing the unavoidable consequences of these choices to teach them the lessons that they might ultimately need to learn.

9. See, for example, C. S. lewis, *Surprised by Joy*.

DISCUSSION QUESTIONS ON CHAPTER 4

(1) In this chapter I have suggested that libertarians and compatibilists can surely agree that moral freedom requires that someone has surpassed a certain threshold of rationality. Do you agree with that claim? If so, why? If not, try to articulate a clear reason why you disagree with it.

(2) An assumption also expressed in this chapter is that both free will and moral responsibility require a causal break of some kind from the past as well as from eternity itself and that indeterminism in human behavior is therefore required in order to provide such a causal break. Do you agree that free will requires such a causal break? If so, why? If not, why not?

(3) Consider the claim that "some of the very conditions essential to our *emergence* as independent rational beings and therefore as free moral agents—conditions that include various degrees of indeterminism—are themselves obstacles to *full* freedom and moral responsibility." Do you agree with that? If so, do you also agree that full freedom and moral responsibility in such cases as the loving mother who cares for her baby and the honest banker who refuses a bribe do not always require the power to act otherwise? Explain your answer.

5

THE TEMPTATIONS
OF FATALISM

DIODORUS CRONUS WAS A young contemporary of Aristotle; and even though none of his own writings are now extant and only tiny fragments of his thought have been preserved in the writings of others, he became famous in antiquity for an attempted refutation of the Aristotelian doctrine of real contingency.[1] According to that Aristotelian doctrine, which is also the view of common sense, "What neither is nor will be is [sometimes] possible"; that is, at least some events that never occurred in the past nonetheless could have occurred, and at least some that will never in fact occur in the future remain possible in the sense that they still could occur. At any given time, therefore, alternative futures remain genuine possibilities. But Diodorus also presented his Master Argument as a refutation of this commonsense view, and his argument included two premises:

1. See Kneale and Kneale, *Development of Logic*, 117–19. The following three quotations in this paragraph are from page 119.

one concerning the necessity of the past, which we already examined back in chapter 2, and one aimed at transferring this necessity of the past to the future. As expressed in his own (translated) words, the first premise thus reads: "Everything that is past and true is necessary"; and the second reads: "The impossible does not follow from the possible." If these two premises are true, he argued, only the actual is genuinely possible and we have no more control over the future than we now have over the past.

Because the second premise, once clarified, turns out to be less controversial than the first, even as some may find it to be the more confusing, we should perhaps clarify it before tackling the more controversial first premise. When Diodorus asserted that the "impossible does not follow from the possible," he gave expression to a correct modal principle, at least as far as *logical* possibility and impossibility are concerned. If a proposition p entails a proposition q (i.e., if q follows from p) and q is itself logically impossible, then p is logically impossible as well. For how could a proposition entail, say, an explicit contradiction unless the proposition that entails this contradiction should include a contradiction as well? But since Diodorus' first premise speaks of necessity rather than impossibility, we can perhaps avoid needless complications at this point by sticking with the concept of necessity, as it appears in the first premise. For even as no logical possibility can entail a logical impossibility, neither can a logical necessity entail a logical non-necessity. What follows from a logical necessity, in other words, must itself be logically necessary.

Now Diodorus' first premise—namely, "Everything that is past and true is necessary"—indicates, first of all, that he had in mind not logical necessity, but the kind of necessity typically attributed to past events and states of affairs; in particular, he had in mind their fixed and unalterable character, as discussed back in chapter 2. His reference to what is *both* past *and* true indicates, secondly, that he probably had in mind true propositions of a certain kind. So let us say that a proposition *p* expresses a fixed and unalterable fact relative to the present time if, and only if, (a) *p* is true and (b) it is metaphysically impossible that someone, even an omnipotent being, should have, either at the present time or at any subsequent time, any further control over whether or not *p* is true. Given this explanation, the principle that Diodorus evidently wanted seems to have been something like this: whatever follows logically from a fixed and unalterable fact about the past is itself a fixed and unalterable fact at the present time. So understood, the second premise of the Master Argument seems perfectly acceptable.

But just how are we to understand the first premise? More specifically, just what might qualify as an example of something that is both "past and true," as Diodorus himself understood it? Consider the proposition, *Lincoln was assassinated in 1865*. This proposition might initially seem like a perfect example of something that is both past and true, because it is clearly about the past, relative to the present time, and clearly true. So whatever one might think about the propriety of locating the truth of a proposition in time, the event that makes this proposition true is, at the present time, already buried in the past and the proposition itself, many people would agree, thus expresses a fixed and unalterable fact in the sense defined above. But since the fact of Lincoln's assassination in 1865 is about the past *exclusively* in the sense that it is consistent with whatever events might (or might not) occur in the future, neither does it have any fatalistic implications. This is not exactly, therefore, what Diodorus had in mind when he spoke of that which is both past and true.

RECONSTRUCTING THE MASTER ARGUMENT

When someone claims that no one, not even God, now has any control over the past, whether it be Lincoln's birth on February 12, 1809, or his assassination on April 15, 1865, this is not to deny, of course, that we may yet have control over various relational facts concerning these past dates—such as the possibility that on February 12, 2029, I might yet have control over whether I celebrate Lincoln's birthday on that date (which is still in the future as I write this sentence) and therefore whether he was born exactly 220 years before I do so. Because such relational facts, insofar as they turn out to be genuine facts, are only *partly* about the past and depend in part upon what happens in the future, they do not, strictly speaking, describe something that is *both* past *and* true in the sense that Diodorus had in mind.

But at this point Diodorus would no doubt argue that even facts about the future are, in an important sense, already located in the past. For if on February 12, 2029, I do celebrate Lincoln's birthday, then it is already true and thus already a fact, Diodorus would likely insist, that this is just what I will do on that date. Here such locutions as "it is already true that" or "already a fact that" seem to suggest that certain truths (or facts) about the future have a metaphysical nature similar to that of an event already buried in the past. For just as no one, not even God, can now exercise any further control over a past event, neither can anyone, Diodorus seems to have believed, exercise any control over the past truth of a proposition about the future. What he evidently had in mind, then, is that a truth (or a fact) about some event in the future, being already located in the past, is itself subject to the necessity of the past and subject to it even before the described future event has slipped into the past. That seems to me the best interpretation of his statement that everything that is past and true is necessary.

In defense of a similar view, Mark Bernstein has written, "If it is true that Jones will meet his grandfather [next] Wednesday, then no one has the power to prevent this meeting. If Jones's being killed [beforehand on] Tuesday would prevent that meeting . . . then he (metaphysically) cannot be killed beforehand."[2] Bernstein then goes on to explain, "The type of necessity that attaches to the fatalist's thesis . . . is the necessity that all past events acquire when they become past."[3] So clearly, Bernstein here treats the truth of a future-referring proposition as if it were itself subject to the necessity of the past even as a past event would be. Similarly, Richard Purtill applies the thesis that the "past cannot be changed" not only to past events, but also to the truth values of propositions about the future. So if "every statement, including any statement about the future, has a truth value," he argues, "one can get a Master Argument type of argument going and reach the conclusion that the future is fixed."[4] Like Diodorus and Bernstein, then, Purtill acknowledges no distinction between what is *merely* true about the future and what is *unavoidably* true about it; he supposes instead that, if a proposition about some future event should be true, then its truth will be subject to the necessity of the past even before the relevant event slips into the past.

These remarks suggest an argument of the following form:

(P1) For any event *e* that occurs at some future time *t*, some proposition of the form: *e occurs at t*, is true and, if you will, true at all times and all places.

2. Bernstein, "Fatalism," 67.

3. Bernstein, "Fatalism," 66.

4. Purtill, *Logic*, 355.

79

(P2) For any event *e* that occurs at some future time *t*, if a proposition of the form: *e occurs at t*, is true at all times and all places, then at no time prior to *t* is it even possible that someone, whether it be God or some creaturely person, should have the power to prevent the occurrence of *e* at *t*.

Therefore,

(C) For any event *e* that occurs at some future time *t*, at no time prior to *t* is it even possible that someone, whether it be God or some creaturely person, should have the power to prevent the occurrence of *e* at *t*.

Stated more informally, (P1) expresses the idea that, for any future event, some proposition that describes it is true; (P2) expresses the idea that every such truth about the future is now unpreventable because, like an event buried in the past, it is already subject to the necessity of the past; and (C) is the validly drawn conclusion that, therefore, every event that occurs in the future is already unpreventable at the present time.

So interpreted, the Master Argument in effect defends fatalism by challenging, among other things, the common-sense idea that any truth about what happens in the future would *depend asymmetrically* upon what actually happens in the future rather than *vice versa*; and because this argument is valid and has two premises, a non-fatalist who rejects its conclusion must be prepared to reject at least one of its two premises. But which one, if either, should a proponent of the commonsense view reject? Those who reject the first premise or (P1), as Bernstein and Purtill both do, reject the whole idea that every well-formed proposition about the future has a definite truth value, either true or false. As Purtill himself has put it, some of these propositions "may have a probability but they do not have *either* the value 'true' *or* the value 'false.'"[5] So the basic idea here is that, yes, all contingent truths or facts about what happens in time depend asymmetrically upon what actually happens in time, not *vice versa*; and yes, what happens at some future time T is what will determine the truth (or the facts) about what happens at T. But that's only because, according to Purtill and others, there are no truths or facts at all about what happens contingently at a specific time T until T becomes present and instantly moves into the past. So at least some well-formed propositions about the future—about future free actions, in particular—are neither true nor false at the present time.

Now those non-fatalists who reject the first premise or (P1) of the above argument typically do so because they have already accepted its second premise or (P2); in that respect, they agree with the fatalist in rejecting any possibility of a distinction between what is *merely* true about some future human action and what is *unavoidably* true about it. Or, to put it another way, they hold that every true proposition about some future event would inevitably express a fixed and unalterable fact about it in the sense defined above. But those non-fatalists who reject the second premise or (P2) above will insist that the mere truth of certain propositions about the future carries no implication of fatalism at all. For if (P2) is false—and, as I suspect, seriously confused—then the possibility remains that not every true proposition about the future will be *unavoidably* true. So herein lies, I believe, the most important philosophical issue that such arguments for fatalism have raised. Are there any good reasons to believe that certain truths or facts about future events, assuming there are such truths or facts, would be subject to the necessity of the past even before the relevant events they describe have slipped into the past? I

5. Purtill, *Logic*, 355 (his italics).

think not, and my reasons for saying this will be discussed further in the following section.

THE FATAL FLAW IN THE MASTER ARGUMENT FOR FATALISM

I have suggested that (P2)—the premise stating that the truth of certain propositions about future events would render these events unpreventable—is seriously confused. But just what is the philosophical confusion I am alleging here? It is akin to what some philosophers might call a category mistake: the failure to appreciate the extent to which the concept of *truth* and that of *an event* signify two very different kinds (or categories) of thing. Even as it makes perfect sense to say that a symphony is in C-sharp minor and no sense at all, outside a special context, to say that the Empire State Building is in C-sharp minor, so it makes perfect sense to say that *an event* occurs at a specific time and place and no obvious sense to say that *the truth about an event* occurs (in the sense of being confined to) a specific time and place. It is therefore important, at the very least, not to treat the truth of a proposition about the future as if it were itself a specific event already buried in the past and thus subject to the necessity of the past.

Consider, by way of illustration, the following proposition:

(P) Mickey Mantle hits a home run in Yankee Stadium on May 22, 1963.

This proposition is *tenseless* in the sense that it provides no indication *via* tense of when 1963 occurs in relation to the present time. It is also *directionless*, as I shall call it, in the sense that it provides no indication of where Yankee Stadium is in relation to where I am now writing this sentence in my hometown of Salem, Oregon. Virtually all of us know, of course, that 1963 is in the past relative to the present time, and many of us also know that Yankee Stadium lies several thousand miles east of Salem. But in any case, what happens in Yankee Stadium on May 22, 1963, I contend, determines whether the tenseless proposition (P) is true at all times and all places or false at all times and all places, and we have no more reason to claim that (P), which we now know to be true, was neither true nor false in 1960 than we have to claim that it is neither true nor false south of Yankee Stadium in Florida but true north of Yankee Stadium in Canada. What more reason do we have to locate the truth of (P) in the past than we have to locate it in a specific place north (or south) of Yankee Stadium?

By way of a response to such questions, Richard Purtill writes:

> Some philosophers have tried to evade the conclusion [of the Master Argument] by arguing that you cannot speak of statements being true *at a time.* But either this creates new problems about how [a] statement can be true without being true at any time *or,* if it is claimed that any statements if true at all are true at all times, we can construct an even stronger version of the Master Argument.[6]

But unfortunately, Purtill provides nary a clue concerning what this stronger argument might be or what might make it stronger; neither does he provide—and this is the more important point—a single reason why we should treat the truth of certain propositions about the future as if such a truth were relevantly similar to a past event or temporal process that would be subject to the necessity of the past. It is easy enough, no doubt, to stipulate some artificial sense

6. Purtill, *Logic*, 354–55.

in which we can locate the truth of a proposition, such as (P), at a particular time and a particular place. Here is how Bernstein does just that:

> We can understand "proposition p is true in place q" as "had anyone uttered in q the sentence that expresses proposition p, he would have expressed a true proposition." Similarly, we can analyze "proposition p is true at time t" as "had anyone uttered at t the sentence that expresses proposition p, he would have expressed a true proposition." In effect, the translation assigns to the moment of utterance the dispositional property of containing a true proposition p had anyone uttered the sentence "p."[7]

So does Bernstein here show that the truth of (P) above belongs to the category of spatial objects, or that it is spatially located in some meaningful sense east of New York in Salem, Oregon? If not, why suppose there to be some meaningful temporal sense in which, even before May 22, 1963, the truth of (P) was already located in the past? It seems to me, at any rate, that Bernstein merely underscores the fundamental difference between an event, which occurs at a specific time and place, and the truth of a contingent proposition, which cannot itself be *confined to* a specific time and place.

Here two points are perhaps in order. First, most people would acknowledge, I presume, that the act of uttering a sentence on some occasion, one that expresses a true proposition, would itself be an event that occurs at a specific time and place. But second, consider also what it means to say that the event described in (P) takes place at a *specific* time? Part of what this means, surely, is that at some other times—even an indefinitely large number of

7. Bernstein, "Fatalism," 71.

them—the same specific event does not take place. So if we say that (P) is true at all times, this is a way of acknowledging that the *truth* of (P), unlike the *event* it describes, cannot be located at, or confined to, any specific time; it is a way of acknowledging, that is, what is correct in the timeless theory of truth. Because the truth of (P), unlike the event that (P) describes, has no *specific* temporal location at all, it is not subject to the necessity of the past until the event it describes, which does have a specific temporal location, slips into the past.

So herein lies, I believe, the answer to a further question that Bernstein raises: "How, precisely, can something that has always been a fact depend upon events that are in our power to perform."[8] Here is the short answer implicit in what we have already said: Just as an event that occurs at a specific place determines what is true about this event at all other places, so *an event that occurs at a specific time determines what is true about this event at all other times*, including all earlier times. Why should the latter claim be any more mysterious than the former? But for a longer answer, recall our explanation back in chapter 2 of why the expression "the necessity of the past" is something of a misnomer and why a more accurate expression might be "the inaccessibility of the past." As we pointed out there, the crucial issue here concerning this inaccessibility is the direction of causation. Insofar as our actions have no effects in the past, we have no control of any kind, not even a compatibilist kind of control, over past events. But our actions unquestionably *do* have effects in the future. So, for that reason alone, we have control over some parts of the future of a kind that we do not have over the past, and God, if he exists, presumably has something akin to an absolute control over the future.

8. Bernstein, "Fatalism," 73.

Note also that the relationship between the truth of a proposition about the future and what happens in the future is not a causal relationship in either direction. Just as the truth about some future event is not itself a cause of that future event, neither is that future event a *causal* condition of the truth about it. We can instead regard the following as a matter of logical or metaphysical necessity: the proposition, *Event E occurs at time T*, is true at all times if, and only if, event E occurs at time T. So, contrary to what Bernstein would have us believe, having control over the truth about some future event in no way "requires the possibility of backward (or retro-) causation."[9] The truth about some future event is not, after all, itself an event or a temporal process standing in a causal relation with other events or temporal processes; so having control over the truth about some future event requires only that one have control over an action that has certain effects in the future. If our freedom with respect to such an action is of a compatibilist kind, then our control over some truth about the future is also a compatibilist kind of control; and that already is a kind of control that we do not normally have over the past. But if our freedom with respect to such an action is of a standard libertarian kind, then our control over some truth about the future is likewise a libertarian kind of control. So yes, such control can be of a kind that includes genuine alternatives at the very time one chooses to act. For whatever explains how one comes to perform an action that has effects in the future will also explain why some proposition about the future is true at all times and true at all places.

One might be inclined to ask at this point, "If the relation between the truth if a proposition about the future and the event it describes is not a causal relation, then how should we understand my previous claim that the truth

9. Bernstein, "Fatalism," 74.

about what happens in time always depends asymmetrically on what actually happens in time? The answer, already implicit in the previous paragraph, is that we have no access to the truth about what happens in time except insofar as we are able to perform actions that have effects in time. If at some future time I will have both the power to do A and the power to refrain from A, then that is just what it means to say that I will then have the power to determine whether some tenseless proposition is true at all times and places or false at all times and places. Or if you prefer, that is just what it means to say that I have the power to bring it about that some tenseless proposition always has been and always will be true. That is just how the concept of *truth* functions in our language and how it differs from the concept of an *event*. So if, either before or after July 21, 2022, someone should guess (without knowing) that it rains on this date in Los Angeles and, as unlikely as rain may seem for this date in Los Angeles, this person should guess correctly, it surely follows that this person has unknowingly asserted a true proposition. For why should a correct guess made after the fact be handled any differently than one made before the fact? Regardless of the time or the place a guess is made, it seems reasonable to say that a guess is correct if, and only if, the one making the guess thereby asserts a true proposition.

Now against my claim that this is just how the concept of *truth* functions in our language, Bernstein replies as follows: "To be told, in effect, that this is just the way some temporally relational facts work, is not to give an answer but to abruptly end the dialogue. The fatalist is not likely to be converted. At this point, the ever-recurring meta-issues regarding burden of proof and question-begging are likely to resurface."[10] But surely the burden of proof always rests squarely on the shoulders of those who claim to have a

10. Bernstein, "Fatalism," 73.

proof, and in our present context it is the fatalist who claims to have a proof of fatalism. So the issue is not whether the fatalist is "likely to be converted" by the non-fatalist's understanding of facts about future contingencies; the issue is whether the fatalist has a strong argument that *ought* to persuade non-fatalists, whether it in fact persuades them or not. In the present context, therefore, the burden rests with the fatalist to answer the following question: How *could* the truth about some future human action depend upon *anything other than* an action that someone has the power to perform? What else could determine the truth value of such a proposition? As for the issue of which side of this controversy, if either, is begging the question against the other side, it is surely Bernstein who begs the question when he assumes, without argument, that the truth of a proposition about the future would be subject to the necessity (or the inaccessibility) of the past even before the event or temporal process that this proposition describes slips into the past. I know of no one who has provided even a remotely plausible answer to such a question as that.

FATALISM AND MODAL CONFUSION

Although no one has yet produced, in my opinion, a single good reason for treating all true propositions about the future as if they were *unavoidably* true as well as *merely* true, some have offered a very confused reason for doing just that. For if a proposition is true at all, some have argued, it cannot also be false; and if it is true even as it cannot be false, then it is necessarily true and thus unavoidably true. As Arthur C. Danto once argued, "since a proposition cannot be both true and false, it *follows* [my emphasis] that if it is true, it cannot be false."[11] And if it is true even as it cannot

11. Danto, *Analytic Philosophy of History*, 188.

be false, then it is necessarily true. So all true propositions are necessarily true.

But that is in fact a textbook example of a fallacious modal inference, one that illicitly transfers the impossibility of a conjunction to one of its individual conjuncts. It also illustrates just how tricky our ordinary modal concepts—the concepts of *possibility*, *impossibility*, and *necessity*—can be in a variety of contexts. Here is how Danto himself spells out his argument in greater detail, using what he calls certain "rules of synonymy":

(1) [A determinate proposition] p is necessarily either true or false.

(2) If p is true, then it is impossible that p is false.

(3) If it is impossible that p is false, then it is impossible that p is not true.

(4) If it is impossible that p is not true, it is necessary that p is true.

∴ (5) If p is true, then it is necessary that p is true.[12]

The confused modal inference in this argument appears in step (2), and the balance of the argument demonstrates conclusively that step (2) is indeed confused. But we need a way of making the confusion here clear to ourselves, and Leibniz's notion of a possible world, as it was refined in the mid-twentieth century, provides a convenient way of doing just that. For although *possible world semantics*, as many philosophers would call it, raises a host of complicated, extremely technical, and even contentious metaphysical issues, none of these need concern us in our present context. As Christopher Menzel points out, "The idea of possible worlds is evocative and appealing,"[13] quite

12. Danto, *Analytic Philosophy of History*, 188. The symbol "∴" in front of step (5) is a commonly used symbol for "therefore."

13. Menzel, "Possible Worlds," third para.

apart from these complications and technical matters; and because fallacious modal reasoning can sometimes appear perfectly reasonable to the unwary, the language of possible worlds can be especially useful in helping to detect and to clarify such fallacious reasoning.

So just how should we understand this idea of a possible world (or a maximal state of affairs, as it is sometimes called)? It is perhaps enough, for our purposes, to think of it as a useful fiction representing any complete way "things as a whole" might have been. The most obvious example of such a possible world would be the *actual world* or the complete way things as a whole in fact are (including everything that has been in the past and everything that will be in the future). But if any aspect of the actual world could have been (or could be) different, then there is another possible world that would realize this difference. So the basic idea here is that every genuine possibility can be thought of as being realized in some possible world, or even infinitely many of them for that matter, whereas every impossible state of affairs, such as a square circle, can be thought of as existing in no possible world at all.

In addition to that, here is what one must understand in order to translate Danto's argument into the language of possible worlds. A *contingent proposition* would be true in some possible worlds and false in others, a *contingently true proposition* would be true in the actual world and false in some other possible world, a *necessarily true proposition* would be true in all possible worlds, and a *necessarily false (or impossible) proposition* would be false in all possible worlds (or true in no possible world at all). With that rudimentary understanding in hand, note how easily the language of possible worlds can clear up the confusion in the inference that Danto draws. For step (2) in his argument above is thus equivalent to

(2*) If p is true in the actual world, then p is not false in any possible world at all.

But if p is a contingent proposition, then (2*) is obviously an invalid inference. So could it be that Danto really meant to say that if p is true in the actual world, then p cannot *also* be false in the actual world? That would at least be a valid deduction from his correct claim that a proposition cannot be both true and false. As already indicated, however, the balance of the argument demonstrates conclusively that this is not what he intended to say. For apart from the invalid inference in (2*), there is no way he could employ such trivial steps as (3) and (4) in order to reach his absurd conclusion, which is equivalent to

(5*) If p is true in the actual world, then p is true in all possible worlds.

But however fallacious such reasoning may be, it can also be highly seductive—so seductive that Steven Cahn actually defined fatalism as "the thesis that the laws of logic alone suffice to prove that no man has free will."[14] By "the laws of logic" he no doubt had in mind a set of formal principles, such as "if p then p" and "either p or *not-p*," that are presumed to be logically necessary. But if that is so, then any argument for fatalism that supposedly rests upon the laws of logic alone will likely include one or more serious modal confusions, as the following passage in Cahn's book illustrates:

> Let us assume that it is true that [a person] M will perform [an action] A at [a time] T. In that case there is no way M can prevent his performing A at T. He may regret that he will perform A at T; he may wish that he could do something to prevent it; but since it is true that he will

14. Cahn, *Fate, Logic, and Time*, 8.

perform A at T, all his efforts to refrain from A
at T will be in vain.[15]

Here Cahn paints a picture of a person M struggling
against the truth that M will do A at T, possibly regretting it
or wishing that he or she "could do something to prevent it,"
even as the truth wins out in the end. But quite frankly, this
is just silly. Cahn ignores altogether the distinction between
whatever effort, if any, that M will in fact expend to refrain
from A at T and the effort he *could* expend toward this end,
and in no way does the picture he paints support his asser-
tion that if "it is true that M will perform A at T," then "there
is no way M can prevent his performing A at T." Granted,
the picture that Cahn paints here would have some point
if we suppose, as he evidently does, that the truth about
what M will do at T, like an event buried in the past, will
already be subject to the necessity of the past prior to the
occurrence of time T. But in addition to our critique of that
supposition in the previous section, the salient point here is
that the laws of logic alone tell us nothing about the nature
of the past and its necessity. So if Cahn intends to argue
from the laws of logic alone for the picture he paints in the
above quotation, then the only explanation left for his argument would be a modal confusion of one kind or another.

Here Cahn may be thinking of an argument similar
to Danto's above, one that illicitly transfers the impossibility of a conjunction to one of its individual conjuncts. But
the above quotation also suggests an argument that illicitly transfers the logical necessity of some conditional as
a whole to its consequent.[16] For the following conditional
is no doubt logically necessary: if it is true that M will do
A at T, then M will do A at T. From that logical necessity,

15. Cahn, *Fate, Logic, and Time*, 10.

16. Every conditional of the form: *if p then* q, has an antecedent
(the if-clause or *p*) and a consequent (the then-clause or *q*).

however, it simply does not follow that, if it is true that M will do A at T, then M's doing A at T would itself be a logical necessity as well. If that were a valid inference, note once again how easily one could "prove" that every true proposition is necessarily true. For every proposition, after all, entails itself; hence, every conditional of the form; *if p then p*, expresses a logical necessity. And it is hard to see how anyone could be fooled by the following kind of argument: any proposition of the form: *if p then p*, is true in all possible worlds; therefore if *p* is true in the actual world, then *p* is true in all possible worlds.

For my own part, at any rate, I cannot think of any reason beyond an obvious modal confusion that would lead someone to accept the thesis that "the laws of logic alone suffice to prove that no man has free will."

CONCLUSION

According to many fatalists, no proposition about some future event can be true at all without also being *unavoidably* true and hence without being in some important sense metaphysically necessary. But the arguments for this conclusion in the existing literature on fatalism seem to be of two kinds: those that commit a category mistake by treating the truth of a proposition about some future event as if it were itself an event or a temporal process already buried in the past and thus subject to the necessity of the past, and those that exhibit a clear-cut modal confusion. We have therefore found no good reason to reject the distinction between that which is *merely true* and that which is *unavoidably true*.

As we shall see in the following chapter, however, the attempt to derive similar fatalistic implications from certain theological assumptions concerning God's existence and foreknowledge of the future cannot be dismissed so easily. For unlike the truth of a proposition about some future event, it is hardly a category mistake to treat a past belief about the future as if it would be subject to the necessity of the past. Still, I shall propose a rather unconventional way of exempting God's past beliefs from the necessity of the past as well as a conception of divine providence that might render the whole issue moot in any case.

DISCUSSION QUESTIONS ON CHAPTER 5

(1) An important issue raised in this chapter is whether the truth of a proposition about some future event would itself be subject to the so-called necessity of the past. But I have argued that, unlike an event or some temporal process that occurs at a specific time and place, the truth of a proposition about some future event is not itself confined in the same way to a specific time and place. It is a simple category mistake, therefore, to treat the truth of such a proposition as if it were itself an event buried in the past and thus subject to the necessity of the past. Do you find that argument persuasive? If so, why? If not, try to explain why the truth of a proposition about some future event must indeed be subject to the necessity of the past.

(2) According to Mark Bernstein, "we can analyze 'proposition p is true at time t' as 'had anyone uttered at t the sentence that expresses proposition p, he would have expressed a true proposition.'" Now certainly the act of uttering a sentence is an event that takes place at a specific time and place even as this same event does not take place at a host of other times and places. But does that provide a single good reason for treating the truth of a proposition about some future event as if

that truth were confined to a past time in a sense that would render it subject to the necessity of the past? Explain your answer.

(3) Another issue raised in this chapter is how easily certain modal confusions may tempt some to accept certain arguments for fatalism. For certain invalid in-ferences—those that illicitly transfer the impossibility of a conjunction to one of its individual conjuncts, for example, or those that illicitly transfer the necessity of some conditional as a whole to its consequent—may appear perfectly valid to the unwary. Do you think that you could explain such confusions to a third party? If so, what sort of explanation would you offer? If not, why not?

6

DIVINE FOREKNOWLEDGE, DIVINE PROVIDENCE, AND HUMAN FREEDOM

ACCORDING TO MANY THEISTS, though by no means all, God's essential omniscience includes an infallible foreknowledge of every future event, including every future human action. So unless one rejects altogether the idea that God holds beliefs about the future in time, one might wonder why God's past beliefs would not be just as fixed and unalterable, relative to the present time, as anyone else's beliefs held in the past would be. As Linda Zagzebski once commented, "a divine past belief seems to be as good a candidate for something as strictly past as anything you can think of—say, an explosion that occurred last week."[1] So the question to be explored here is whether, given such infallible foreknowledge, God's past beliefs about the future would transfer the fixed and unalterable character of the

1. Zagzebski, "Recent Work on Divine Foreknowledge," 55.

past to the future. If so, then it may look as if something like the Master Argument would be sound after all, at least in the case of a God whose foreknowledge of the future is infallible.

As already mentioned, not all theists hold that God's omniscience includes an infallible foreknowledge of the future. In addition to the classical idea of God's timelessness, according to which God's infallible beliefs about some temporal event cannot be located in time either before or after the event in question occurs, a growing number of theists today, the so-called open theists, simply deny that God has an infallible foreknowledge of our future free actions and they do so without making any appeal to the doctrine of divine timelessness. They argue instead that, as an omniscient being, God knows all that is possible to know and they go on to deny that an infallible foreknowledge of someone's future free actions is a possible form of knowledge.

So that raises the obvious question of whether one could both sidestep the whole controversy over divine foreknowledge and maintain a robust understanding of divine omniscience by simply placing God and his cognitions in a timeless realm where there is no such thing as a past, a present, or a future. At the very least, that would avoid the claim that God's infallible beliefs about our future actions would be subject to the supposed necessity of the past. But the doctrine of divine timelessness also raises a host of complicated and exceedingly confusing issues. One of these, though not one particularly relevant to the free will controversy, is whether a timeless knower could know what time it is right *now*, or know whether Lincoln's assassination is *now* in the past, is *now* presently occurring, or is *now* in the future. Such a being could certainly know that Lincoln's birth occurs some fifty-six years before his assassination and that his birth is therefore in the past *in relation to* that assassination. But if the flow or passage of time is a genuine metaphysical reality—if, that is, whatever exists contingently comes into being in an objective present, a present that continues moving into what just was the future a few seconds ago, so that whatever happens in the present immediately starts receding into the past—then it follows, some have argued, that a timeless knower would have no way of knowing what point in the timeline of world history this objective present has in fact reached.[2]

More relevant to the free will controversy, perhaps, is the claim of several recent philosophers that a timeless realm would have the same kind of ontological necessity as the past does. In the words of Linda Zagzebski, the "timeless realm is as much out of our reach as the past."[3] So why is that? She elaborates as follows:

> Surely the timeless realm is as ontologically determinate and fixed as the past. Perhaps it is inappropriate to say that timeless events are now necessary. Even so, we have no more reason to think that we can do anything more about God's timeless knowledge than about God's past knowledge. If there is no use crying over spilt

---

2. In opposition to such an argument, Katherine Rogers writes: "It is often said that a timeless God cannot be omniscient because He cannot know what time it is now. But this criticism presupposes the essentially tensed view of time [or what many philosophers would call the A-theory of time]. On the tenseless view [or the B-theory view] it is true that God cannot know what time it is at some italicized 'now,' but that is because there is no such thing. . . . [In other words,] there simply is no ontologically privileged now. It is our limited perspective which leads us to believe that there is" (see Rogers, "Anselmian Eternalism," 12–13). It is obviously well beyond the scope of this chapter to get into the weeds on this controversy. But for a good introduction to some of these issues, see chapter 9 "Temporal Passage" in the fourth edition of Richard Taylor, *Metaphysics*, 80–87.

3. Zagzebski, "Foreknowledge and Free Will," 2.2.

> milk, there is no use crying over timelessly spill-
> ing milk either.[4]

I find these remarks to be as instructive as they are perplexing. They are perplexing because the very idea of a timeless event seems to be an incoherent idea. Is it not true by definition, as we saw in the previous chapter, that events take place at a specific time and place? And even if we think of a timeless act of creation, one that results in, among other things, a first moment of time, as an exception to this, what could the expression "timelessly spilling milk" (as op-posed to "a timeless knowledge of someone spilling milk at a specific time and place") possibly mean in the present context? We certainly have no reason to deny that a cor-rect recollection of my having spilt milk at a specific time and place depends asymmetrically on what happens at that specific time and place; and neither do we have, so far as I can tell, any reason to deny that God's timeless knowledge of such an event would likewise depend asymmetrically on what happens at the relevant time and place.

Still, the above remarks nonetheless strike me as instructive for the following reason. Apart from a clear understanding of why the past ordinarily remains so inac-cessible to us and therefore seems to be so "ontologically determinate and fixed," we have no way to assess accurately whether the same kind of reasons would apply either to a set of timeless beliefs or even to all of God's own past beliefs (if he should indeed have such past beliefs). So having already examined the necessity of the past back in chapter 2, let us now examine more closely a traditional understanding of God's infallible foreknowledge and some of the unique characteristics traditionally attributed to it.

4. Zagzebski, "Recent Work on Divine Foreknowledge," 52.

Consider Zagzebski's suggestion that, even if one "can produce an account of temporal asymmetry that has the consequence that God's past beliefs do not have the necessity of the past, it is unlikely that this can be done in a way that is independently plausible."[5] For in order for such an account "to be convincing," she insists, we need "some account of God's belief states that makes it intuitively plausible to think of a temporal deity as independent of the modalities of time aside from our interest in resolving the foreknowledge problem."[6] But when addressing the foreknowledge problem, we surely can (and should), as I presume Zagzebski would agree, take into account any unique facts about God and his "belief states" that might be relevant to the issue. For unlike our own beliefs buried in the past as well as an explosion that occurred last week, God's past beliefs are no more a part of his creation than, as Creator, God himself is part of it. And whereas we would expect an explosion that occurred last week to be explicable in terms of ordinary laws of nature, we would not expect this of God's past beliefs about contingent events in the future.

Suppose it should turn out, then, that the laws of nature governing God's creation should exclude the very possibility of backward (or retro-)causation, where an effect would precede its cause in time. This might preclude a case of precognition among human beings where, as some have imagined, a later event causes and thus brings about an earlier act of precognition. But it would not preclude the possibility that God has a unique ability to look into the future course of events within his creation without affecting any of these events at all. Neither would it preclude the possibility of a free person freely performing an action A that

5. Zagzebski, "Recent Work on Divine Foreknowledge," 54–55.
6. Zagzebski, "Recent Work on Divine Foreknowledge," 55.

actually brings about a prior belief (or even an everlasting belief of a tenseless kind) in the God who foresees it. For as we already saw back in chapter 2, Zagzebski herself points out—correctly in my opinion—that "the necessity of the past may simply be the principle that past events are outside the class of causable events." It is the normal direction of causation—the fact that our actions have effects in the future but no (obvious) effects in the past—that makes the past seem so utterly *inaccessible* (and therefore closed) to us. And because our actions unquestionably do have effects in the future, there is, as I shall try to demonstrate in the following section, a seemingly plausible way to reconcile divine foreknowledge with human freedom and to exempt at least some of God's past beliefs from the so-called necessity of the past.

HOW TO EXEMPT GOD'S PAST BELIEFS FROM THE NECESSITY OF THE PAST

I begin with an analogy that makes no reference to any temporal asymmetries at all. Suppose that I should produce, either by drawing it or in some other way, an equilateral triangle on a blank sheet of paper. Here is a necessarily true bi-conditional, call it (BT), concerning such triangles:

(BT) A triangle is equilateral if, and only if, it is also equiangular.

Because (BT) is necessarily true or true in all possible worlds (see the previous chapter), these two facts—the fact that a given triangle is equilateral and the fact that it is also equiangular—are in that sense metaphysically equivalent facts; and from this equivalence it follows that any action of mine that brings about an equilateral triangle on a page will also bring it about that an equiangular triangle is on the same page. It is simply logically (or metaphysically) impossible that I might draw the one without also drawing the other.

So now consider a very traditional conception of God, according to which, as a non-contingent or a necessary being, God exists in all possible worlds and all of his perfections, including omniscience, are essential properties as opposed to mere accidental properties. The distinction here between essential and accidental properties is just this: whereas the accidental properties of something are those it lacks in at least some of the possible worlds in which it exists, its essential properties are those that it possesses in every world in which it exists. So God is a being who exists in all possible worlds and is omniscient in every world in which he exists. The traditional conception of God's omniscience includes, moreover, the idea that at any given time God has a perfect foreknowledge of every future event; and given that conception, the following bi-conditional concerning God's past beliefs about the future, call it (BG), is likewise metaphysically necessary or true in all possible worlds:

(BG) God believes at a time T_1 that an event E will occur at a time T_2 if, and only if, E does in fact occur at T_2.

From the metaphysical necessity of (BG) together with the fact that our actions, so we believe, have effects in the future, it immediately follows that at least some of God's past beliefs remain accessible to us in an important sense in which other past events and states of affairs do not. For suppose that I should toss a rock into a calm lake and that event E is the subsequent disturbance in the water, which occurs at time T_2. It surely is plausible to say that my act of tossing a rock into the lake brings about the relevant disturbance in the water that occurs at T_2. So given the traditional conception of God sketched above and its implication that (BG) expresses a metaphysical necessity, the following surely is a plausible argument. Even as an action of mine cannot bring about an equilateral triangle on a page without also bringing it about that an equiangular triangle is on the same page, neither can an action of mine bring about a disturbance in the lake water at T_2 without also bringing it about that God believes at an earlier time T_1 that this disturbance will occur at T_2.

Lest there should be any confusion in the matter, I should perhaps make an additional clarification at this point. In calling the above an "independently plausible" account of why at least some of "God's past beliefs do not have the necessity of the past," I do not mean to imply that it is somehow a *decisive* account. If God should causally determine, either directly or indirectly through secondary causes, my act of tossing the rock into the lake, then in a more fundamental sense it would be God who brings about this act of mine as well as the relevant disturbance in the water at T_2; and if God intended from the beginning to cause all of this to happen, then his foreknowledge of what would happen at T_2 may simply rest upon his own intention to act in a certain way. But if God does not causally determine this act of mine, what else except my tossing a rock into the lake at T_2 *could* explain God's belief at T_1 that the relevant disturbance in the water would occur at T_2? My point is that, given that (BG) is not only true but necessarily true, whatever provides an ultimate explanation for why the disturbance in the water occurs at T_2 will also explain why God holds the relevant belief that he holds at T_1.

Now some might persist in asking at this point, "How *could* God foreknow that some contingent event, one that he does not fully control himself, will occur at some specific future time?" My short answer to this question would be that I have no idea. Neither do I have any idea of how God could create the universe *ex nihilo*, as many theists believe he did. But the issue now before us is not whether we can fully understand how God could foreknow some aspect of the future without controlling it; the issue is instead whether anyone has provided a single good reason for the claim that God's prior beliefs obtained through his foreknowledge, however infallible they may be, would have to be fixed and unalterable in the sense defined back in chapter 2. Merely to repeat the expression "the necessity of the past," as a kind of shibboleth at this point, is hardly to provide a genuine reason. For given that God's past beliefs obtained through his foreknowledge of the future (a) are not themselves part of the created order, (b) are not themselves the product of any backward causation *within the created order*, (c) cannot be explained in terms of any created laws of nature, and, finally, (d) are the product of a unique ability to view the future unfolding before him, none of the factors that make the past seem so inaccessible to us are even relevant to these particular beliefs. Instead, these beliefs would depend upon what happens in the future in exactly the same way that the truth of a future-referring proposition depends upon what happens in the future.

Accordingly, with respect to the aforementioned example of my causing a disturbance in the calm lake water, let us now suppose that I both have the power to throw that rock into the lake at T_2 and have the power to refrain from doing so. No one denies that this would be both the power to bring about a disturbance in the lake water and the power to prevent *this particular* disturbance in the water (caused by a rock that I fling into the lake). So if I freely exercise my power to bring about this disturbance in the water, in no way would that preclude my also having an unexercised power to prevent this particular disturbance from occurring. Similarly, if I freely exercise my power to bring it about that God has always believed that this disturbance in the water would occur at T_2, in no way would that preclude, especially given (BG) above, my also having an unexercised power to bring it about that God has always held a very different belief concerning this matter.

FOREKNOWLEDGE AND GOD'S PROVIDENTIAL CONTROL OF OUR LIVES

Although divine foreknowledge poses no threat whatsoever to human freedom, at least not so far as I can tell, some theistic philosophers have worried—for good reason, I believe—that even a perfect foreknowledge of the future would contribute little or nothing, by itself, to God's providential control of our lives. The basic reason for this, as William Hasker has explained, is that "when God *foresees* a particular event occurring it is 'too late,' in the order of explanation, for God to determine either that it *will* or that it *will not* occur."[7] For God could hardly foreknow that an event will occur in the future if that event will not in fact occur in the future. So insofar as God should rely upon a simple foreknowledge of our free choices and rely upon that alone, he would be a *dependent knower*; it would be as if he looks into the future and thereby discovers what these free choices will be. There would be no time, it is true, when God is ignorant of what these choices will be, but neither could his decision to permit a given situation to arise in the first place, or to permit a free choice to be made in it, be based on an a "prior" knowledge of what that choice will be. God's foreknowledge of our free choices would thus be like a discovery, though not one made at a specific time. Call it an *eternal* discovery, if you will.

7. Hasker, "Divine Knowledge and Human Freedom," 49.

But why, one might ask at this point, should anyone have ever supposed that a mere foreknowledge of the future would suffice for a robust providential control over our lives anyway? Part of the *historical* answer may lie in the fact that certain biblical texts, which many Christians take to be authoritative, may initially appear to specify a link between a strong conception of divine providence, such as someone being foreordained or predestined to a glorious end, on the one hand, and some sort of divine foreknowledge, on the other. A prominent example I saw referenced many times during my own youth was St. Paul's declaration in Romans 8:29 that reads as follows: "For those whom he [God] foreknew he also predestined to be conformed to the image of his Son, in order that he might be the first-born among many brethren" (RSV) But here it is *persons* who are foreknown, not their future free choices; to be foreknown in this sense is simply to be an object of God's redemptive love from the very beginning of creation itself.

Note also that later in the letter Paul used the same word when he wrote, "God has not rejected his people whom he foreknew" (Rom 11:2); and it seems obvious from the context of this latter text that Paul here had in mind all the descendants of Abraham, including those disobedient ones, as Paul understood them to be, who had temporarily rejected Christ and were thus blinded or hardened at the time of Paul's writing (11:7). That he had in mind a mere temporary setback, one that in no way counted against the guarantee of their ultimate inclusion and restoration (see 11:12) is made abundantly clear when Paul immediately insisted that they had not stumbled so as to fall (11:11). To the contrary, their stumbling would eventually result, he insisted, in the salvation of all Israel (11:26)—that is, of all the descendants of Abraham—including those who had been blinded or hardened for a season. For what could be clearer than this? "As regards the gospel they [i.e., the disobedient descendants of Abraham] are enemies of God for your sake; but as regards election they are beloved for the sake of their ancestors; for the gifts and the calling of God are irrevocable" (11:28–29). Then, just in case you miss the underlying principle here, Paul immediately generalized his specific point and applied it to the human race as a whole, both Jews and gentiles: "For God has bound everyone over to [their own] disobedience so that he may have mercy on them all" (11:32—NIV). In some mysterious way, Paul thus claimed, our own acts of disobedience, however freely performed, will contribute, as an expression of God's merciful providential control of our lives, to our ultimate deliverance from sin and death.

So was Paul here claiming that divine providence somehow depends upon a foreknowledge of our future free choices? Hardly. It depends instead upon the way in which God employs the consequences of our free choices, whichever way they go, as a means of perfecting us in the end. Just as a grandmaster in chess can know without doubt that he will eventually checkmate a novice, regardless of which moves the novice makes along the way, so God will eventually win over the most hardened of sinners, Paul seems to be saying, regardless of which choices they make along the way (see the following section). Call this *a kind* of foresight, if you will. But it is not a kind that would require a detailed foreknowledge of every future event. As Linda Zagzebski once pointed out, moreover, it seems "unlikely that the historical motive [or the most important philosophical motive] for affirming infallible foreknowledge was that it is necessary for divine providence";[8] many theistic philosophers, after all, seem to have affirmed such foreknowledge "because it was thought to be an aspect of

8. Zagzebski, "Recent Work on Divine Foreknowledge," 61.

cognitive perfection and hence a requirement for a perfect being."[9] In any case, as Hasker puts it in a section heading, "Foreknowledge Is Not Enough"—not enough, that is, for a robust providential control of history. But again, I ask, why should anyone ever have thought otherwise?

Now one way in which theistic philosophers have sought to combine human freedom with a more robust divine providence is to claim that, in addition to an in-fallible foreknowledge of the future, God's omniscience includes what many now call middle knowledge: a perfect knowledge of what every possible person would do in any possible set of circumstances in which that person has the power to act freely. The basic idea here is that, for every possible person S and every possible set of circumstances C in which S has a free choice to make, there are true subjunc-tive conditionals of the following form: *If S should be in C, then S would freely do A in C.* Although all of these true sub-junctive conditionals are known to God, their truth value is also independent of God's will and helps to determine what God's options are in creation. So the upshot is that God knows from the beginning what any possible person would do freely if God should choose to create that person and to place that person in a set of circumstances involving a free choice of some kind or another. God even knows, therefore, how Hitler would have turned out had he been, among many other differences from his actual history, acci-dentally switched as a newborn baby and raised in a loving Jewish family.

But there is, not surprisingly, a huge debate over the issue of whether middle knowledge is a genuinely possible form of knowledge. For the record, I personally have a strong sense—which is hardly a decisive argument, if any argument at all—that middle knowledge is not a genuine

9. Zagzebski, "Recent Work on Divine Foreknowledge," 61.

possibility, particularly in certain extreme cases. If C is a set of circumstances in which S has both the power to do A and the power to refrain from A and C obtains, then what happens in C can determine, in the sense previously explained in chapter 5, what always has been and always will be the truth about what happens in C; it can also explain why God always has and always will believe the truth about what happens in C. But if C never obtains or, worse yet, S never even exists, then what is it that grounds the truth concerning what would have happened if C had obtained? Nothing, so far as I can tell.

Fortunately, however, we need not try to resolve such issues here, and I am quite content to let the chips fall where they may on the issue of whether there is such a thing as an infallible divine middle knowledge. According to Hasker, "It is plausible that Molinism [the view that God does have middle knowledge] offers the only feasible way to combine a traditional strong view of divine providential control with the libertarian free will that many find essential."[10] But as we saw back in chapter 4 and elsewhere, even libertarian free will requires a minimal degree of rationality; and as we saw back in chapter 1, not even a categorical power to choose otherwise can turn an utterly irrational choice into a genuinely free choice. So whether or not God in fact has middle knowledge, the fact that our freedom in relation to God requires a minimal threshold of rationality—that fact alone—opens the door to many forms of providential control, as we shall see. How robust such a providential control may be, or whether it can guarantee a glorious end for any given individual, are matters we shall explore further in the following section.

10. Hasker, "Divine Knowledge and Human Freedom," 50.

DIVINE PROVIDENCE AND HUMAN FREEDOM

Is there a way in which divine providence could *both* accommodate the kind of indeterminism that human freedom requires *and* continue to teach us over an indefinitely long period of time all of the lessons we need to learn for our own good? I believe there is. For given a widely accepted theological assumption concerning the divine nature and its relation to human happiness and human misery, God could, so it seems to me, *guarantee* a glorious end for even the most determined and hardened of sinners, however filled with hatred for God they may be at some given time, simply by permitting them to experience the very condition of separation that they have freely and confusedly chosen for themselves.

So just what is this widely accepted theological assumption that I here have in mind? Concerning the divine nature, C. S. Lewis once wrote that "union with that Nature is bliss and separation from it [an objective] horror."[11] But that no doubt raises this further question: just what would constitute a *complete* separation from the divine nature of an omnipresent God? Or, to put it another way, how should we understand the logical limit of any such separation from the divine nature? A number of recent theists have suggested that the annihilation of hardened sinners would constitute the logical limit of such separation even as it would avoid the monstrosity of a supposed eternal torment in hell. But as an interpretation of the Lewis remark, that will never do. For once an individual center of consciousness has been annihilated, it would no longer have the capacity to experience anything whatsoever, including any sense of horror in being separated from the divine nature. Although the annihilation of someone we love may indeed seem horrible to

11. Lewis, *Surprised by Joy*, 232.

those of us who are still alive, it could hardly seem horrible to someone who has already been annihilated. So insofar as the intended contrast that Lewis had in mind was between the *experience* of bliss, on the one hand, and the *experience* of an objective horror, on the other, the annihilation of an individual could hardly be part of this intended contrast.

How, then, *should* we understand the relevant idea of being separated from God? In his great sermon "The Consuming Fire," George MacDonald employed the biblical language of being "cast into the outer darkness" (see Matt 8:12; 22:13; 25:30 KJV) to describe the logical limit of separation from God as far as he thought this to be possible *short of being annihilated altogether.* Here is how he described the sheer horror of such a separation from God and from all that God does to make a life worth living:

> Imagination cannot mislead us into too much horror of being without God—that one living death. . . . For let a man think and care ever so little about God, he does not therefore exist without God. God is here with him, upholding, warming, delighting, teaching him—making life a good thing to him. God gives him himself, though he knows it not. But when God withdraws from a man [or the man withdraws from God] as far as that can be without the man's ceasing to be; when the man feels himself abandoned, hanging in a ceaseless vertigo of existence upon the verge of the gulf of his being, without support, without refuge, without aim, without end, . . . with no inbreathing of joy, with nothing [including the faintest experience of love] to make life good, then will he listen in agony for the faintest sound of life from the closed door . . . .[12]

12. MacDonald, "Consuming Fire," 31.

In the context of these remarks, MacDonald also described the outer darkness as "a terrible doom" that awaits anyone who might be cast into it; and like many Christian theologians, he seems to have regarded this terrible doom as a feature of the afterlife, where there will be greater clarity insofar as many of the ambiguities and misperceptions of our earthly lives will already have been cleared away. The twofold assumption here is that our freedom in relation to God will continue into the afterlife and that the consequences of our free choices there will be more immediate, more obvious, and much less subject to self-deception than they now are in this life. In fact, it is, according to MacDonald, precisely those who continue resisting the consuming fire of God's love in the lake of fire (a symbol for divine judgment in the afterlife) who are at the greatest risk of being cast into the outer darkness. So we could just as easily understand the outer darkness as a symbol for how, as a last resort, God could simply permit the most hardened of sinners to experience the very life apart from God that they have confusedly chosen for themselves. Understood in that way, the outer darkness would seem to be something akin to a soul suspended alone in sheer nothingness, without even a physical order to experience.

Now that would certainly be an objective horror, one that would immediately shatter any illusion that a life apart from God and apart from the goods that only he can provide might be a life worth pursuing. God would thus have a kind of trump card to play as a last resort in the afterlife, if he should in fact deem it necessary to do so for our own good: just permit us to experience the very condition of separation that we might freely, albeit confusedly, have been moving toward throughout our lives. Far from interfering with our freedom in relation to God, this trump card would enable God to respect our own free choices even as he uses them to teach us some of the hardest lessons we may need to learn. But because separation from God can also be a matter of degree and the relevant choices are inevitably made in a context of ignorance and illusion, I have serious doubts whether the infinitely resourceful God would ever find it necessary to play this particular trump card that he continues to hold in reserve, so to speak. For most of us make a vast number of significant choices throughout our earthly lives and perhaps even into the afterlife—choices whose consequences inevitably correct various degrees of ignorance and shatter many illusions that we may have had at one time or another. Still, the important point here is that no one could *both* experience the horrific nature of the outer darkness, as MacDonald described it above, *and*, after learning from experience its true nature, continue to embrace it freely.

As further support for this claim, consider two very different ways in which God, conceived of as an omnipotent and perfectly loving Creator of the universe, might interfere with a creature's freedom to perform some specific action. Imagine that a man is standing atop the Empire State Building with the intent of committing suicide by jumping off and plunging to his death below. One obvious way in which God might interfere with this man's freedom to kill himself would be simply to cause him to change his mind; that would effectively prevent the suicide from occurring. But there is another, less obvious, way in which God could interfere with the man's freedom to commit suicide. God could permit him to leap from the building and then cause him to float gently to the ground like a feather; that too would effectively prevent the suicide from occurring. So this man is not free to perform his intended action of committing suicide unless God permits him to achieve his intended goal, and neither are the most hardened of sinners free to live apart from God, or apart from the ultimate source of human happiness as many theists understand it, unless God permits them to experience the very life that they have chosen along with the full horror that such a life might entail.

But if that is true, how could even the most hard-hearted of sinners *both* freely separate themselves from the divine nature in the outer darkness *and* freely choose to remain in such a state of separation forever? Either God could permit such sinners to follow a path that ultimately leads, according to many theologians, to an objective horror and permit them to continue following it for as long as they freely choose to do so, or God could at some point prevent them from continuing along their freely chosen path. If God should permit sinners to continue along their freely chosen path—the one that unbeknownst to them will inevitably lead them to an objective horror—then their own experience, provided they are rational enough to qualify as free moral agents, would eventually shatter the illusions that made their misguided choices possible in the first place. It would also enable them to begin appreciating, as they continue to learn lessons from the consequences of their own actions, why union with the divine nature is indeed preferable to the horror of a separation from it. Over time that would enable them to begin appreciating, as they continue to learn lessons from the consequences of their own actions, why union with the divine nature is indeed preferable to the horror of separation from it. Alternatively, we might imagine that God should surreptitiously prevent sinners from achieving their freely chosen goal, perhaps by shielding them from the horror of a life without any implicit experience of the divine nature. But if God should do that—if, as George MacDonald has put it, he should continue to give these sinners himself, though they know it not—then they would have no real freedom to continue separating themselves from the divine nature. In neither case, therefore, could sinners retain forever their power to continue separating themselves from the divine nature and from the ultimate source of human happiness.

In conclusion, if our freedom in relation to God requires that we have surpassed a minimal threshold of rationality, as I have argued, then God's providential control of our lives need not rest upon his foreknowledge of the future and need not require anything like middle knowledge. For a good deal of such providential control could be built right into God's original design of his creation. With respect to those, such as small children, who have not yet surpassed the minimal threshold of rationality, or those, such as victims of Alzheimer's disease, who have fallen well below that minimal threshold, or those, such as certain drug addicts or even the hard of heart, whose own misguided choices have rendered their own behavior utterly irrational—with respect to all of these, God would know that nothing he might do to improve their cognitive faculties or to meet the relevant threshold of rationality could interfere with some nonexistent freedom. And with respect to those who are indeed rational enough to qualify as free moral agents, God would know that they will eventually learn all of the lessons they need to learn if he permits them to experience the very life they keep confusedly choosing for themselves.

Here is why. Essential to the whole corrective process is that we exercise our moral freedom—not that we choose rightly rather than wrongly, but that we choose freely one way or the other. We can choose today to live selfishly or unselfishly, faithfully or unfaithfully, obediently or disobediently. But our choices, especially the bad ones, will also have unintended and unforeseen consequences in our lives; as the proverb says, "The human mind plans the way, but the LORD directs the steps" (Prov 16:9). For our bad choices in particular never get us what we really want; that is part of what makes them bad and also one reason God is able to bring redemptive goods out of them, if he should choose to do so. When we make a mess of our lives and our misery becomes more and more unbearable, the hell we thereby create for ourselves will in the end resolve the very ambiguity and shatter the very illusions that made the bad choices possible in the first place. That could be how God works with us as created rational agents. He could permit us to choose freely in the ambiguous contexts in which we first emerge as self-aware beings, and he could then require us to learn from experience the hard lessons we sometimes need to learn. So in that way, the consequences of our own free choices, both the good ones and the bad ones, could be a source of revelation; they could reveal sooner or later—in the next life, if not in this one—both the horror of separation from God and the bliss of union with him. And that is how the end could be foreordained: all paths could finally lead to the same destination, the end of reconciliation, even if some should turn out to be longer, windier, and a lot more painful than others.

DISCUSSION QUESTIONS ON CHAPTER 6

(1) One of the more controversial suggestions made in this chapter is that, unlike our own past beliefs and an explosion that occurred last week, God's past beliefs are no more a part of the created order and no more subject to the laws of nature governing that created order than God himself is part of the created order or subject to the laws of nature governing it. But our actions clearly do have effects in the future. So given the assumption that our actions have no effects in the

past and given the necessity of (BG) above, it imme-diately follows that at least some of God's past beliefs are now accessible to us in a way that other past events in the created order are not. Does that argument make any sense to you? If so, try to express the gist of it in your own words. If not, try to state an objection to it as clearly as you can.

(2) According to a number of theistic philosophers, God's omniscience includes middle knowledge, which is a knowledge of what any free person, whether this per-son ever exists or not, would have done in any possible situation, including one that never actually obtains. Assuming a libertarian conception of freedom, does it seem to you as if this is a possible form of knowledge? If not, why not? If so, is there some truth of the mat-ter, in your opinion, about what a person would have done freely in a possible situation that never obtains? Explain your answer.

(3) Consider just one aspect of the divine knowledge— namely, the perfect knowledge that God would have at each present moment of every detail of his creation in that moment, including each person's present desires, intentions, motives, ignorance, faulty judgments, il-lusions, and the like. Do we have any reason to deny that this knowledge alone would suffice for a robust providential control over our lives? And given that our freedom in relation to God requires a minimal thresh-old of rationality, do we have any reason to doubt that God could, if he so chose, teach us all of the lessons we need to learn for our own good and could do so without interfering with our freedom in relation to him? Explain your answer to these questions.

SUMMARY AND CONCLUSION

HAVING REVIEWED A NUMBER of the philosophical issues and controversies that have arisen in recent decades on the topic of free will, I have sought to do so without concealing my own opinions and biases on this topic. But neither would I want to conceal the fact that much more could be said on both sides of the various issues that we have covered.

In any event, the perspective I have expressed here concedes to incompatibilists that free will could never exist in a fully deterministic universe; and if a supremely powerful Creator of our universe should causally determine every event that occurs in it, as some theological determinists hold, then only one independent being capable of free action would exist, namely, the Creator who is causally responsible for everything that happens in the universe. But the perspective expressed here also concedes to the compatibilist that, if someone's decision-making process includes any element of indeterminism, then that indeterminism would constitute an element of random chance of a kind that can reduce both the degree of one's responsibility for the decision made and the degree of the freedom that one has in making it. So is my claim here that free will is incompatible with both determinism and indeterminism and that it is therefore an incoherent concept? Not quite. My claim is instead that indeterminism is a necessary condition of someone's *emergence* as a free moral agent—in part because it provides the necessary causal break from the past and from the causal activity of any deity, if one should exist. But such indeterminism is also an *obstacle* to *full* freedom and moral responsibility, both of which require, as an additional necessary condition, a minimal threshold of rationality. Moral freedom requires, in other words, that one be rational enough to begin learning important lessons from the consequences of one's own choices (or quasi-choices).

Beyond all of that, I have set forth the following sufficient condition of acting freely: someone who qualifies as an independently rational creature, as defined in chapter 4, acts with some degree of freedom whenever it lies within one's power to follow one's own reasonable judgment concerning the best available action in a given situation; indeed, the power to act freely just is the power to exercise such rational control over one's own actions. So free will does not always require the power to act otherwise, particularly when so acting would be utterly irrational—as when, for example, someone finds it psychologically impossible to do something that seems utterly unthinkable, unspeakably evil, or in some other way horrific. With respect to this power to act otherwise, however, we have found no good reason to believe that such a power would be incompatible either with all genuine propositions having a definite truth value or with an omniscient God having a perfect foreknowledge of the future. Still, on the assumption that a supremely powerful and supremely loving God does exist, our free choices and the lessons we continue to learn from the consequences of these free choices are what would determine the shape of the future and would thus explain God's foreknowledge of it, not *vice versa*. So it would be God's ability over an indefinitely long period of time to teach us all the lessons we need to learn, not his foreknowledge or even some kind of middle knowledge (if there is such a thing, which I doubt), that would explain God's providential control of our lives and the guarantee it provides that his creation will eventually come to a glorious end. Put it this way: such a God, if he should exist, would have the power, whether he should choose to exercise it or not, to bring about a glorious end for us regardless of which way our free choices happen to go in any situation in which we have the power to choose otherwise.

So now I would invite readers of this book to formulate your own arguments against any aspect of the perspective on free will that I have set forth here.

SUGGESTIONS
FOR FURTHER READING

THE PHILOSOPHICAL LITERATURE ON free will is vast and varied; and from that vast sea of literature, some of it highly technical and exceedingly complicated, I here select a few items that seem especially relevant to issues raised in the text and are not already included in the bibliography of works cited. For the most part, my sense of what might be appropriate for an undergraduate philosophy class on the topic of free will has guided the selections I have made below.

A. J. Ayer, "Freedom and Necessity." In *Philosophical Essays*, 271–384. New York: Macmillan, 1954. Online: https://commonweb.unifr.ch/artsdean/pub/gestens/f/as/files/4610/006166_111415.pdf. Written with exquisite clarity, this classic defense of compatibilism appears in a number of anthologies, including the first edition of *Free Will*, edited by Gary Watson (Oxford: Oxford University Press, 1982). Although it was dropped from the second edition, the above URL should enable this article to be read online.

C. A. Campbell, "In Defence of Free Will." The Inaugural Address, Glasgow University, 1938. Online: https://www.informationphilosopher.com/solutions/philosophers/

campbell/defence.html. This inaugural address, delivered at Glasgow University, is an especially clear and compact defense of the simple libertarian view, as we called it in chapter 1. But unlike others who hold this view, Campbell also restricted the categorical power to do otherwise to cases where someone experiences a conflict between inclination or desire, on the one hand, and a sense of moral obligation, on the other. And whatever one might think of such restrictivism in the end, it seems to help in clarifying the categorical power to act otherwise, as Campbell himself understood it.

Richard Double, *The Non-Reality of Free Will*. New York: Oxford University Press, 1991. Although Richard Double concludes, reluctantly, that free will is impossible, some of his arguments against the libertarian view also illustrate why I have contended that some of the very conditions essential to our own emergence as free moral agents—such conditions as indeterminism, ignorance, and a context of ambiguity and misperception—are also obstacles to a fully realized freedom.

Laura W. Ekstrom, "Free Will Is Not a Mystery." In *The Oxford Handbook of Free Will*, 2nd ed., edited by Robert Kane, 366–80. New York: Oxford University Press, 2011. This article is especially relevant to chapter 3 because Ekstrom here distinguishes between different senses of the term "chance" in an effort to combat the claim that indeterminism implies sheer randomness.

William Hasker, *God, Time, and Knowledge*. New York: Cornell University Press, 1989. Hasker here sets forth a powerful case for the view that divine foreknowledge is incompatible with human freedom, which is in fact a view that I try to counter in chapter 6 under the heading "How to Exempt God's Past Beliefs from the Necessity of the Past."

Robert Kane, *A Contemporary Introduction to Free Will*. New York: Oxford University Press, 2005. Robert Kane is a giant in the community of those philosophers who have published on the topic of free will, and probably no one has a more comprehensive grasp of the scholarship in this field than he does. Remarkably, he also has a talent for expressing technical and complicated arguments in a way that makes them altogether accessible to beginning students. So even though I personally remain highly skeptical concerning his understanding of certain "voluntary 'self-creating' or 'self-forming' actions," this book is nonetheless a powerful resource for beginning students.

Alfred R. Mele, *Free Will and Luck*. New York: Oxford University Press, 2006. Although aimed at a professional audience, this book is quite readable and is, beyond that, especially relevant to our chapter 4 for the following reason: the sufficient conditions of acting freely that Mele sets forth—slightly altered for the libertarian, on the one hand, and for the compatibilist, on the other—all include, as does ours set forth in chapter 4, a rational judgment that some action is the best thing to do in a given situation. Also, Mele's concluding chapter or chapter 8 clearly summarizes the book as a whole and the relevant sufficient conditions of acting freely.

Robert Nozick, "Choice and Indeterminism." In *Agents, Causes, and Events: Essays on Indeterminism and Free Will*, edited by Timothy O'Connor, 101–14. New York: Oxford University Press, 1995. Best known, perhaps, for his libertarian *political* philosophy, Robert Nozick here provides a fascinating, subtle, and highly readable defense of a libertarian conception of free will—which is not, of course, a political philosophy at all.

Eric Reitan, "A Guarantee of Universal Salvation?" *Faith and Philosophy* 25.4 (2007) 413–32. Online: https://www.pdcnet.org/collection/fshow?id=faithph il_2007_0024_0004_0413_0432&pdfname=faithph il_2007_0024_0004_0049_0068.pdf&file_type=pdf . Without making any appeal ether to divine foreknowledge or to middle knowledge, Eric Reitan here illustrates a very simple way in which divine providence could, with a near mathematical certainty, guarantee that every free person would *freely* choose communion with God in the end. For a brief summary of the argument, see section 4.2 of the entry entitled "Heaven and Hell in Christian Thought" in *The Stanford Encyclopedia of Philosophy* at the following URL: https://plato.stanford.edu/entries/heaven-hell/#UniandHumFree.

Michael Scriven, "Responsibility." In *Primary Philosophy*, 198–228. New York: McGraw Hill, 1966. Here Scriven sets forth a clear and succinct defense of the claim that moral responsibility and the freedom it requires is compatible "with brain determinism" and with a scientific explanation of human behavior.

Peter Van Inwagen, "The Incompatibility of Free Will and Determinism." *Philosophical Studies* 27 (1975) 185–99. Published earlier than *An Essay on Free Will* and slightly less technical, this article is also reprinted in *Agency and Responsibility: Essays on the Metaphysics of Freedom*, edited by Laura Waddell Ekstrom, 17–37. Boulder, CO: Westview, 2001.

BIBLIOGRAPHY
OF WORKS CITED

Almeida, Michael, and Mark Bernstein. "Rollbacks, Endorsements, and Indeterminism." In *The Oxford Handbook of Free Will*, 2nd ed., edited by Robert Kane, 484–94. New York: Oxford University Press, 2011.

Bernstein, Mark. "Fatalism." In *The Oxford Handbook of Free Will*, edited by Robert Kane, 65–81. New York: Oxford University Press, 2002.

Cahn, Steven M. *Fate, Logic, and Time*. New Haven, CT: Yale University Press, 1967.

Danto, Arthur C. *Analytical Philosophy of History*. New York: Cambridge University Press, 1968.

Dennett, Daniel. *Elbow Room: The Varieties of Free Will Worth Wanting*. Cambridge: MIT Press, 1984.

Double, Richard. *Metaphilosophy and Free Will*. New York: Oxford University Press, 1996.

Edwards, Jonathan. *Freedom of the Will*. Online: https://www.apuritansmind.com/wp-content/uploads/FREEEBOOKS/TheFreedomoftheWill-JonathanEdwards.pdf.

Ekstrom, Laura Waddell. *Free Will: A Philosophical Study*. Boulder, CO: Westview, 2000.

Frankfurt, Harry. "Alternative Possibilities and Moral Responsibility." *Journal of Philosophy* LXVI (1969) 829–39.

Hasker, William. "Divine Knowledge and Human Freedom." In *The Oxford Handbook of Free Will*, 2nd ed., edited by Robert Kane, 39–54. New York: Oxford University Press, 2011.

Kane, Robert. "Responsibility, Luck and Chance: Reflections on Free Will and Indeterminism." In *Agency and Responsibility*, edited by Laura Waddell Ekstrom, 158–80. Boulder, CO: Westview. 2001.

———. *The Significance of Free Will*. New York: Oxford University Press, 1998.

Kapitan, Tomis. "A Compatibilist Reply to the Consequence Argument." In *The Oxford Handbook of Free Will*, 2nd ed., edited by Robert Kane, 131–50. New York: Oxford University Press, 2011.

———. "A Master Argument for Incompatibilism?" In *The Oxford Handbook of Free Will*, edited by Robert Kane, 127–57. New York: Oxford University Press, 2002.

Kneale, Martha, and William Kneale. *The Development of Logic*. New York: Oxford University Press, 1966.

Lewis, C. S. *Miracles: A Preliminary Study*. New York: Macmillan, 1975.

———. *Surprised by Joy: The Shape of My Early Life*. New York: Harcourt Brace Jovanovich, 1955.

MacDonald, George. "The Consuming Fire." In *Unspoken Sermons*, 18–33. Whitethorn, CA: Johanneson, 2004.

Mavrodes, George. "Is the Past Unpreventable?" *Faith and Philosophy* 1.2 (1984) 131–36.

Menzel, Christopher. "Possible Worlds." In *The Stanford Encyclopedia of Philosophy* (Fall 2021 ed.), edited by Edward N. Zalta. <https://plato.stanford.edu/archives/fall2021/entries/possible-worlds/>.

Nowell-Smith, P. H. *Ethics*. Baltimore: Penguin, 1954.

O'Connor, Timothy. *Persons and Causes: The Metaphysics of Free Will*. New York: Oxford University Press, 2000.

O'Connor, Timothy, and Christopher Franklin. "Free Will." In *The Stanford Encyclopedia of Philosophy* (Fall 2018 ed.), edited by Edward N. Zalta. https://plato.stanford.edu/archives/fall2018/entries/freewill/.

Plantinga, Alvin. *God, Freedom, and Evil*. Grand Rapids: Eerdmans, 1977.

Purtill, Richard L. *Logic: Argument, Refutation, and Proof*. New York: Harper & Row, 1979.

Rogers, Katherine A. "Anselmian Eternalism: The Presence of a Timeless God." *Faith and Philosophy* 24.1 (2007) 3–27.

Schlick, Moritz. *Problems of Ethics*. Translated by David Rynin. New York: Prentice Hall, 1939.

Sennett, James F. "Is There Freedom in Heaven?" *Faith and Philosophy* 16.1 (1999) 69–82.

Speak, Daniel. "The Consequence Argument Revisited." In *The Oxford Handbook of Free Will*, 2nd ed., edited by Robert Kane, 115–30. New York: Oxford University Press, 2011.

Stump, Eleonore. "Augustine and Free Will." In *The Cambridge Companion to Augustine,* edited by Eleonore Stump and Norman Kretzmann, 124–47. Cambridge: Cambridge University Press, 2001.

Taylor, Richard. *Metaphysics.* 4th ed. Englewood Cliffs, NJ: Prentice Hall, 1992.

Timpe, Kevin. *Free Will: Sourcehood and Its Alternatives.* New York: Bloomsbury Academic, 2013.

van Inwagen, Peter. *An Essay on Free Will.* Oxford: Clarendon, 1983.

———. "Free Will Remains a Mystery." In *The Oxford Handbook of Free Will*, edited by Robert Kane, 158–77. New York: Oxford University Press, 2002.

———. "Some Thoughts on *An Essay on Free Will.*" *Harvard Theological Review* XXII (2015) 16–30.

———. "When Is the Will Free?" In *Agents, Causes, and Events: Essays on Indeterminism and Free Will*, edited by Timothy O'Connor, 219–38. New York: Oxford University Press, 1995.

Vargas, Manuel. "The Trouble with Tracing." *Midwest Studies in Philosophy* 29 (2005) 269–79.

Wick, Warner. "Truth's Debt to Freedom." *Mind: A Quarterly Review of Psychology and Philosophy* 73 (1964) 527–37.

Williams, Bernard. "Moral Luck." In *Moral Luck: Philosophical Papers 1973–1980*, edited by Bernard Williams 20–39. New York: Cambridge University Press, 1981.

Wolf, Susan. *Freedom within Reason.* New York: Oxford University Press, 1990.

Zagzebski, Linda. "Foreknowledge and Free Will." In *The Stanford Encyclopedia of Philosophy*, edited by Edward N. Zalta (Spring 2021 ed.). https://plato.stanford.edu/archives/spr2021/entries/free-will-foreknowledge.

———. "Recent Work on Divine Foreknowledge." In *The Oxford Handbook of Free Will*, edited by Robert Kane, 45–64. New York: Oxford University Press, 2002.

INDEX